GROWING YOUR OWN VEGETABLES

AN ENCYCLOPEDIA OF COUNTRY LIVING GUIDE

GROWING
YOUR OWN
VEGETABLES

Carla Emery & Lorene Edwards Forkner

SASQUATCH BOOKS
SEATTLE

Portions of this book have appeared, in the same words or in substance, in *The Encyclopedia of Country Living, 10th Edition* (Sasquatch Books, 2008).

Printed in the United States of America
Published by Sasquatch Books
Distributed by PGW/Perseus
15 14 13 12 11 10 09   15 14 13 12 11 10 9 8 7 6 5 4 3 2 1

Cover illustrations: Clipart.com/2009© Jupiterimages Corporation
Cover design: Jennifer Shontz, Red Shoe Design; based on *The Encyclopedia of Country Living, 10th Edition* cover design by Kate Basart/Union Pageworks
Interior design and composition: Jennifer Shontz, Red Shoe Design
Interior illustrations: Clipart.com/2009© Jupiterimages Corporation
Map (page 22): Courtesy arborday.org; copyright © 2006 by The National Arbor Day Foundation

Library of Congress Cataloging-in-Publication Data
Emery, Carla.
  Growing your own vegetables : an Encyclopedia of country living guide / Carla Emery and Lorene Edwards Forkner. — 1st ed.
     p. cm.
  Includes bibliographical references and index.
  ISBN-13: 978-1-57061-570-2
  ISBN-10: 1-57061-570-5
  1. Vegetable gardening—North America. 2. Organic gardening—North America. I. Forkner, Lorene Edwards. II. Emery, Carla. Encyclopedia of country living. III. Title.
  SB324.3.E44 2009
  635—dc22
                         2008050030

Sasquatch Books
119 South Main Street, Suite 400
Seattle, WA 98104
(206) 467-4300
www.sasquatchbooks.com
custserv@sasquatchbooks.com

For Mom and Dad, who allowed me to dig up our backyard, plant corn, and walk away. The weeds grew tall, but the seed for my love of gardening was sown. I can't remember if we got any corn.

—LEF

CONTENTS

Introduction ix

PART ONE: CREATE A GARDEN 1

    Planning Your Garden 3

    Garden Layout 13

    Gardening Under Cover 17

    Planting Dates 21

    Care and Feeding of the Garden 25

    Garden Competition 37

PART TWO: GUIDE TO VEGETABLES 43

    The Onion Family 51

    Leaves 59

    Stems and Flowers 73

    Roots 85

    Grasses and Grains 101

    Legumes 115

    Gourds 123

    The Nightshade Family 133

    Herbs 145

Carla's Legacy 163

Acknowledgments 165

Appendix: How to Maximize Your Garden's Yield 167

Bibliography 171

Index 173

INTRODUCTION

Carla Emery first began to pen what was to become *The Encyclopedia of Country Living* in 1970 while working a small farm in Idaho and parenting the first of her seven children. All around her people were going "back to the land," trading city life for country living. Their desire for self-sufficiency vied with a nagging fear of nuclear annihilation, and they were filled with urgent questions as to how to proceed in their new rural world. Over the years, what had begun as serial chapter installments, produced by hand and mailed to people who responded to an advertisement for an "Old Fashioned Recipe Book" in *Organic Gardening* magazine, grew to become a definitive work on country living and modern homesteading. Now in its tenth edition, thirty-five years after the first complete book was collated (by hand) in a rural library in Idaho, *The Encyclopedia of Country Living* remains a living history and comprehensive resource for "living off the land and doing it yourself."

My journey through its nine-hundred-and-some-odd pages, along with my research and ruminations as to who Carla was, reveals her to have been a remarkable, feisty woman who above all cared for her family and for cultivating a good and healthy life in an independent manner.

She was passionately committed to providing wholesome food produced in an environmentally sensitive way and living in concert with the land and the seasons. Although she may have farmed her many acres in a lifestyle more in keeping with the early twentieth century, in many ways she was not so very different from today's concerned twenty-first-century world citizen looking for good, clean food sustainably produced in a way that supports fair living conditions and a safe environment.

From asparagus to zucchini, this book is largely in Carla's voice and, I hope, communicates her passion, her quirks, and above all her encyclopedic knowledge of living a resourceful, respectful, and responsible country life. What follows is not merely a comprehensive list of vegetables suitable for backyard cultivation, but also the knowledge and details from the ground up to successfully grow your own food. In her inimitable exhaustive way—always categorizing, listing, and enumerating—Carla offers up many choices, alternatives, and options—spinach or chard, draft horse or tiller.

Today's markets are treasure stores stocked with shrink-wrapped, waxed, stacked, and labeled produce shipped from New Zealand, Chile, Mexico, and other distant fields. The fluorescent-lit aisles of these trade giants are a Neverland where one can have summer in the depths of winter, seduced by giant shiny red strawberries in December, and convenient prewashed, carved, and packaged "baby" vegetables. Indisputably, a diet rich in colorful and nutritious vegetables throughout the year is a boon to our health. But look beyond self-interest to examine the industrial complex necessary to support today's megamarts, and you'll find a seamy underbelly fraught with pollution, waste, and human rights abuse. Routine recalls and health warnings remind us that even fresh farmed food is not without health perils.

The cottony disappointment of deceptively red strawberries in winter, sticker shock at the checkout stand, and a desire for wholesome, healthy food has many of us looking for another way. We have choices. Carla would say we are blessed with choices. Many towns and cities now regularly support seasonal farmers markets, community gardens provide growing space for those without access to land, and lucky is the person who has generous neighbors with an abundant harvest. There is a dawning movement toward procuring local foods that follow the rhythm of the seasons—that is, the seasons of the hemisphere in which we reside—and, for those of us looking to participate in a practice nearly as old as the human race, even in our own immediate zip code.

Passionate gardeners, avid cooks, enthusiastic eaters—we're all after the same thing, whether we work a remote farm in the heartland, reside in small towns or suburban developments, or are homesteaders of the last urban frontier, making our home in the city's industrial spaces and dense downtown environments. Our gardens may be measured in acres, patches, backyard plots, community lots, or containers on a fire escape, rooftop, or shyly proportioned balcony. You don't need an acre, a backyard, a garden, or even your own container of dirt to eat good healthy fresh vegetables. But for those of us willing to brave the weather; dance an evasive tango with pests and disease; kneel in the dirt; sport definitely non-fashion-forward tan lines, while shading our heads against the midday sun; or support friends, neighbors, and small farmers who do, the table is set for a feast that feeds both body and mind, belly and spirit, at once economically sound and emotionally satisfying. Discovery and wonder, as well as the occasional disappointment and frustration, await us in each new season in a constantly revolving and delicious trip around the sun.

—Lorene Edwards Forkner

April 2009

PART ONE

CREATE A GARDEN

PLANNING YOUR GARDEN 3

Available Sunlight and Water 4

Plot Size and Shape 5

    Beginning and/or container garden 5

    Experienced gardener with a small garden 6

Warm-Season versus Cool-Season Plants 7

    Gardening in the Deep South 7

Perennials 8

Garden Record Keeping 8

    Sample Garden Record 9

GARDEN LAYOUT 13

Row Planting 14

Raised Beds and Wide Rows 15

"Hill" Planting 16

GARDENING UNDER COVER. 17

    Types of Garden Coverings. 18

        Cloche 18

        Cold frame 18

        Greenhouse 19

PLANTING DATES 21

    Climate Zones 22

    Growing Season 23

    Starting Transplants 23

CARE AND FEEDING OF THE GARDEN 25

    Soil Composition. 25

    Compost and Manures 28

        Compost. 28

        Manure 29

        Green manure 30

    Earthworms 30

    Mulching 33

    Soil Nutrients. 34

GARDEN COMPETITION. 37

    Weeds 37

    Garden Pests Large and Small 39

        Problem mammals 39

        Slugs, snails, and insects 40

        Crop rotation and management 41

PLANNING
YOUR GARDEN

W hether you have an acre in the country, a corner of a suburban backyard, a plot in a community garden, or several containers on the patio or fire escape, if you really want to have a garden, you can! Gardening is fun, educational, profitable—and popular for those very good reasons. For every dollar you spend on your garden you'll get back many times that in delicious, healthy, organic food. It's a good investment of your time too. In addition to the value of your produce, gardening is good for you, body and soul— working your muscles, exercising your brain, and reconnecting you to the vital process of raising nourishing food. With advance planning and by properly locating your garden for the best results, you'll reap generous rewards and a healthy harvest.

AVAILABLE SUNLIGHT AND WATER

Select a potential garden space that receives at least six hours of direct sun a day; although some plants will flourish in partial shade, most need a generous dose of sun. Some gardens may be limited by their water supply or by how far a water source can reach. Plants can absorb food from the soil only if it is in solution—in effect, plants must be damp to grow. Unless you live in an area with dependable, abundant spring-to-fall rains, don't plan to garden vegetables beyond the reach of your irrigation system.

Most vegetables are about 85 to 90 percent water and require generous and faithful watering throughout the season. The best time to water is in the morning. Plants do most of their growing during the day and need water for photosynthesis. Watering in the morning also allows plants to dry out by evening, which reduces the chance of mildew and rot. Almost all vegetables produce better with abundant water; once stunted by drought, many vegetables will not recover. Count on providing about an inch of water a week from nature or your irrigation system. Hook up your water system or drag a hose out into your proposed garden space to verify its range and confirm that you have both water and sunshine!

Know your irrigation system: how fast water is delivered and how fast the soil can absorb it. Surface runoff, puddling, and evaporation are wasteful. In situations where the land is too wet, you may have to design a ditching system to take water off or a levee system to keep it out. Vegetables will not grow under poor drainage conditions. Know your garden and watch the weather, working with it and not against it.

PLOT SIZE AND SHAPE

Gardeners fortunate enough to have plenty of land and time can make their plots any size they wish, limited only by the number of people to be fed and what they like to eat. However, most people have space constraints or are limited by the amount of time they have to maintain a big garden. Gardens can be any shape—a formal four-square, an irregular plot, or a series of smaller beds or containers that can be tucked into even the smallest landscape.

Beginning and/or container garden

The following crops are suitable for a beginning gardener with a small garden or several large containers. This garden will produce many months of good fresh food, beginning with lettuces and green onions in spring followed by a continuous harvest of the other vegetables through summer until frost.

- Bush beans
- Bush peas
- Leaf lettuce
- Onions from sets
- Summer squash
- Swiss chard (no spinach)
- Tomatoes (climate permitting)

Experienced gardener with a small garden

Practiced gardeners with a year or so under their belts may want to expand their crops and their delicious harvests to include a wider range of root crops and longer-season vegetables, as well as some novelties thrown in for fun. *Choose compact varieties wherever possible.*

- Beans, bush and pole
- Brussels sprouts
- Cabbage
- Carrots
- Corn, sweet
- Cucumbers
- Hearty greens
- Herbs
- Kale
- Onions, green and bulbing
- Peas
- Peppers
- Popcorn, dwarf
- Potatoes
- Radishes (red/white)
- Salad garden, including lettuces
- Tomatoes

WARM-SEASON VERSUS COOL-SEASON PLANTS

When planning crops, take your climate into consideration. Tomatoes, eggplant, peppers, melons, and cucumbers are warm-season crops that simply won't grow well until the days are hot. They are injured or killed by frost, and their seeds won't come to life in cold soil. On the other hand, cool-season crops like lettuce, spinach, carrots, and broccoli thrive in wet, chilly spring weather, producing flowers and seeds when the weather turns hot. Cool-season plants generally produce a crop of leaves, roots, or stems, while most warm-season crops produce seeded fruits. (See also the appendix on page 167 for more information.)

Gardening in the Deep South

The extreme heat and humidity of summer in the south can make gardening a real challenge. Smart southern gardeners plan their crops to mature in the more moderate temperatures of fall, winter, and spring, save for the following truly heat-tolerant vegetables:

- ▶ Beans, runner
- ▶ Chard
- ▶ Collards
- ▶ Corn
- ▶ Eggplant
- ▶ Jicama
- ▶ Melon
- ▶ Okra
- ▶ Peas, pigeon and southern
- ▶ Peppers
- ▶ Squash
- ▶ Sweet potatoes
- ▶ Tomatoes

PERENNIALS

Perennials are plants that come back all by themselves year after year. It's wonderful to be able to go out and harvest without having to plant every year! Rhubarb, asparagus, Jerusalem artichokes, fruit and nut trees, berry bushes and strawberries, certain onions, garlic, and many herbs are perennials. When planting perennials, it's important to place them at the edge of the garden or identify an orchard or berry patch, so that when you work the soil each spring you can do so without harming permanent plantings.

GARDEN RECORD KEEPING

Your first garden is the hardest one to plan because everything is theoretical. To plan subsequent gardens, simply adapt the plan used in the previous year, making changes based on what you have learned. It helps to keep weekly notes on a big calendar with plenty of space to write. Keep your records going all summer, even during the busy growing and harvesting months; if you wait until winter to think about lessons learned from the previous summer, you may forget an important note for the coming year. In fact, it helps to do a preliminary plan of your next year's garden each fall while the current growing season is still fresh in your mind.

Your garden records become a valuable tool and offer perspective as you discover that no two gardening years are alike. Weather changes, pest populations fluctuate; even your choice of what to grow will vary. After two or three seasons you will begin to see patterns emerge, and over time you'll grow to understand the conditions unique to your garden.

Sample Garden Record

1. Varieties planted

2. How much seed you used and how much garden space you were able to plant with it

3. Problems encountered—poor germination, insects, disease, bad weather

4. When you began to harvest

5. The yield from each crop

6. Any changes to be made

TEN SECRETS TO GETTING THE MOST FROM A SMALL GARDEN

1. Make use of semishaded areas unsuitable for tomatoes, squash, or melons by growing leafy vegetables like lettuce, chard, mustard, or endive.

2. Make room for herbs, which contribute a broad range of flavors and variety in a relatively limited growing area.

3. Avoid sprawling varieties. You can plant six rows of carrots, beets, or onions in the same square footage occupied by one row of squash vines; choose compact, "bush" varieties of melons, squash, cucumbers, and pumpkins.

4. Consider planting fast-maturing vegetables in the space between slower-maturing ones that will later spread; for instance, plant radishes or lettuce between vine plants like squash or pumpkin for a quick crop before the neighboring plants need the space.

5. Give preference to continuously bearing vegetables. You can continue to harvest chard throughout the growing season long after spinach has gone to seed with the onset of hot weather. Other continuously bearing crops are beans, broccoli, brussels sprouts, cucumber, eggplant, kale, peppers, squash, and tomatoes.

6. Double cropping will give you the greatest productivity per square foot when you plant another crop as soon as you've harvested the previous one, keeping your garden in constant production. Double cropping is most effective with a long growing season, but in most places peas, lettuce, radishes, beets, and carrots mature quickly enough that you have time for a second crop if you plant as soon as the first is harvested.

7. Harvest daily to maximize your garden's production. Many plants—such as beans, broccoli, chard, cucumbers, and summer squash—will stop producing if the plants aren't kept picked.

8. Encourage your garden to grow up rather than out by taking advantage of vertical growing space; train vines on supports to free the space at their feet for other crops.

9. Plant tall crops, such as corn or sunflowers, on the north end of the garden so they don't shade other plants.

10. Practice deep watering, which will encourage roots to go down rather than spreading sideways, allowing you to space plants closer together.

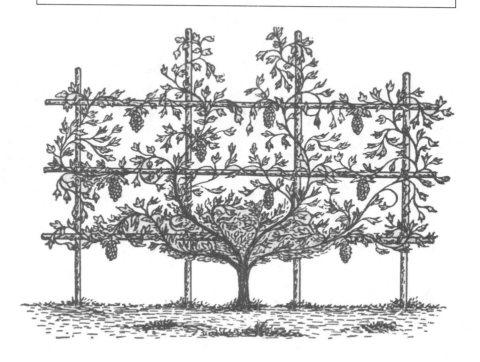

GARDEN LAYOUT

It's time to plant the garden—or more accurately, it's time to plan how to arrange the plants in the garden space. Path placement should take into account not only access to and movement around the garden but also adequate width to allow back-saving wheelbarrow access and power tool maneuvering. Consider whether you will be planting in rows or establishing raised beds. In a sloping garden, it's a good idea to create raised beds with shallow retaining walls to prevent soil erosion. The loss of topsoil to erosion is an irreversible tragedy; it takes nature thousands of years to restore fertile conditions. If you garden or farm on a slope or in an exposed windy location, you can help prevent erosion by using summer mulches, winter cover crops, and grass planted in strips across slopes, as well as strategically placed diversion ditches to direct water flow.

ROW PLANTING

Spacing between rows should be determined by how you plan to cultivate the soil and control weeds. Traditionally, rows were spaced 30 inches apart because a horse pulling the cultivator needed that much space. A smaller garden that is cultivated by hand will accommodate rows as little as 1 foot apart.

DRAFT HORSES AND POWER TOOLS

A horse can outpull a little tractor any day of the week. A single horse can pull 16-foot logs; a team of horses can pull a ton for a short distance, and they can easily pull 300 pounds all day long. Remember to stop and rest often. There is an old saying that if you want to have a good pulling horse, always leave one pull in him. In other words, quit working him while he is still pulling.

Practice is important for any draft animal. Hitching up the animals and using them every day helps them stay at their best and keeps you in practice too. When you are first training draft animals to pull, load them very lightly. Gradually, over time, increase the load. Pat the animal and let it know you appreciate it after a good hard pull. That moment of sincere thanks really makes a difference in the quality of future performance you'll get. On a very hot day, remember both you and your horses require a break with water and shade.

If you plan to use power tools, the space between rows must be wide enough so a tiller can get between them without damaging the plants. One objection to the rototiller is that, like all machines, it's not sufficiently discriminating and can't go around a lovely volunteer that has planted itself right in the middle of the row nor can it easily navigate curves. However, long, straight rows that have been preplanned to be wide enough to accommodate the tiller do make cultivating this way a breeze.

RAISED BEDS AND WIDE ROWS

Evenly spaced but dense plantings in long narrow beds, raised or at grade, make the most of limited space for good growing efficiency. The whole garden or just a part of it may be put into raised beds or wide rows. Whether you are setting out transplants or planting from seed, raised beds or wide rows are spaced so that the plants' outer leaves will touch as they mature to form a dense mass of plants. Thus the growing area is maximized and soil moisture is preserved in the resulting shaded soil.

HOW TO MAKE A RAISED BED

1. Lay out an area 3 to 4 feet wide and as long as you want. Your width is limited by your ability to reach the center of the bed from each side to weed, thin, or harvest as needed; when planning length, consider path placement for easy movement among the beds.

2. Cover the area with 6 inches of aged manure or compost and deeply dig in by hand or with a power tool. After digging, let the bed settle for a few days.

3. Scatter organic amendments over the now raised surface of the bed and rake to break up clods as you mix it into the top 3 to 6 inches. Soak with a gentle spray to prepare for planting.

"HILL" PLANTING

Position plants in clusters, at intervals along a row, with the soil between them kept as clear of weeds as possible. Sometimes the soil is hoed up from every side to make a literal hill about 6 inches higher than the surrounding grade. In very dry areas, hill planting can be modified to create a depression in the ground that will collect and hold water. Hill planting is especially valuable in desert areas and where hot, drying winds blow. In such a climate, the middle plants of the cluster—the most protected ones—may produce the best yield.

GARDENING UNDER COVER

When a cat lies in a pool of sunlight that is streaming through a glass window on a cold but sunny day, it's taking advantage of a natural phenomenon. The radiant energy of the visible sunlight becomes heat energy when it strikes the cat's fur and other surfaces inside the room. Some of this heat is reflected and radiated into the air inside. This heat cannot easily pass back through the glass, so the air inside the window is warmed.

A covering over a garden bed acts in the same manner. When light strikes plants and the soil heat is trapped, the environment within the covered space is warmed. This warmth speeds up all life processes, including the growth and development of garden plants. A garden under cover is protected from rain, frost, wind, and cold. For fall and winter gardening in chilly or cold climates and for very early spring growing, cover is essential. Any structure or device that allows light to enter and protects from cold may be used for gardening under cover.

TYPES OF GARDEN COVERINGS

Cloche

A lightweight, completely transparent covering for a plant or plants that can easily be moved about the garden. A cloche is the simplest cover to build and use although they are vulnerable to heavy wind and do not provide as much protection from cold as cold frames or greenhouses.

The word *cloche* ("klosh") is French for bell, and it well describes the glass jars French market gardeners used to protect their plants. Today, cloches for individual plants may be made of waxed paper, plastic, fiberglass, or glass. A plastic-covered tunnel or tent and floating row covers that protect an entire row of plants offer the protection of a cloche on a larger scale. Floating row covers are made from a very lightweight spun material and can be used to cover plants without any supporting structure; that is, they "float." A wide variety of cloches are available commercially, with an equally wide range in prices.

Cold frame

Consisting of a glass or clear plastic window hinged to an opaque bottomless box, a cold frame is placed directly over a part of the garden, in effect creating an area of milder temperatures within. The hinged lid opens to provide ventilation and allow you to work with your plants; when closed, it protects the plants against cold.

Amend the soil within the cold frame with compost and plenty of organic material to boost fertility and provide drainage. A cold frame is primarily used during the fall, winter, and early spring when the sun is at a lower angle. To capture the available light and heat, site the frame where it will receive full sun between 9 a.m. and 3 p.m., with the long axis of the structure oriented east–west.

The addition of a 6- to 8-inch layer of horse, chicken, or rabbit manure turns the cold frame into a *hotbed*, warming the soil considerably as the manure ages—a boon in cold climates. Carefully monitor conditions within the cold frame to regulate temperature and humidity, and water the plants as needed.

Greenhouse

A glass- or plastic-walled building large enough for people to stand and move around in. Greenhouses can extend the living space of a home while at the same time expanding the garden and provide winter shelter for tender plants. Solar greenhouses rely strictly on the power of the sun for heat.

ADVANTAGES TO GARDENING UNDER COVER

Flexibility in Planting and Harvest Dates—It is discouraging to set out plants only to see them killed by a frost or watch them sit, not growing, until warm weather finally arrives. On the other hand, it is more than a little disappointing to nurse tomato plants through summer only to see the fruit destroyed by an early fall frost or rainstorm. Gardening under cover allows you to adapt seed packet planting and harvest dates to your particular garden conditions.

More Crop Variety—Many less hardy vegetable and ornamental plant varieties can be successfully grown under cover that normally would not do well in your area.

Faster Plant Growth—Robust, unhampered growth results in sturdier plants better able to resist disease and survive bad weather. You can grow more food in less time from the same bit of garden space, and there is even evidence that your crops will taste better.

Less Insect Damage—Early-spring and late-fall plantings avoid garden pests that are not actively feeding in these "shoulder" seasons.

PLANTING DATES

When to plant will vary drastically depending on which hemisphere you live in, altitude, climate, and finally the plant itself. Become an expert on your local climate. Check weather forecasts daily during the growing season to anticipate expected high and low temperatures.

CLIMATE ZONES

The United States Department of Agriculture has developed a map that divides the country into zones determined by a range of minimum temperatures for each specific geographic region. The USDA map has gained nearly universal acceptance; the zones are often referred to in garden books and on plant labels and seed packets to indicate a plant's hardiness.

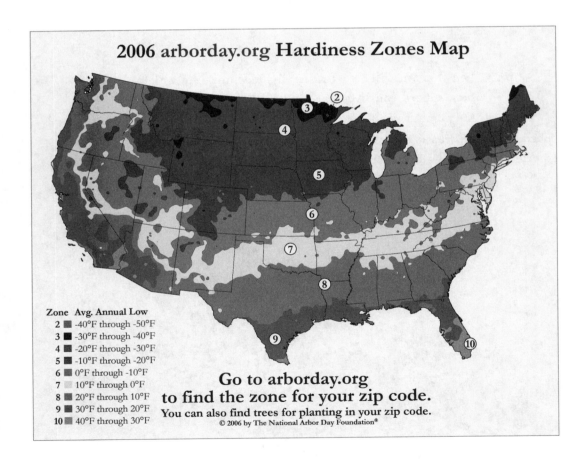

2006 arborday.org Hardiness Zones Map

Zone	Avg. Annual Low
2	-40°F through -50°F
3	-30°F through -40°F
4	-20°F through -30°F
5	-10°F through -20°F
6	0°F through -10°F
7	10°F through 0°F
8	20°F through 10°F
9	30°F through 20°F
10	40°F through 30°F

Go to arborday.org
to find the zone for your zip code.
You can also find trees for planting in your zip code.
© 2006 by The National Arbor Day Foundation®

GROWING SEASON

Broadly determined by the number of days between the last killing frost in the spring and the first killing frost in the fall, your garden's growing season will be further influenced by its topography and exposure. These are important dates for planning when to plant. Most knowledgeable nurseries or a local extension agent will be able to give you estimated dates for the average spring and fall frost dates for your area. Refer to your personal garden records for specific data about your garden.

STARTING TRANSPLANTS

Growing your own transplants allows you to increase the size of your harvest and/or lengthen your growing season and opens up a wide world of varieties not necessarily available at your local nursery. Start your plants about 2 to 2½ months before you plan to set them out. Because most seeds require much warmer soil to germinate than they need to grow, sow your seeds in the house or a heated greenhouse, where you can give them ideal conditions in their tender early stages. Transplants don't need much space; you can grow them on a sunny windowsill. To make room for more plants, build shelves across the window, being careful to remove anything underneath that could be harmed by dripping water.

Fill your containers to the top with a sterile seed starting mix, tamping the dampened soil lightly. Water newly planted seeds often enough to keep the soil continually moist to encourage rapid germination. Peat pots, available at most nurseries, are a favorite seeding container because the entire plant, pot and all, can be placed in the garden to minimize transplant shock. However, plants in peat pots dry out fast; when setting them into the garden, you should tear off the part of the rim that's above ground to prevent it from acting as a wick, causing the plant to lose water. Look around and be resourceful; any container that will hold soil can be used to start transplants, provided you poke holes in the bottom for drainage. *Note: Be sure to label each container with the variety of plant in it.*

Water the seedlings every other day, or whenever they look dry, by thoroughly misting the surface of the soil with a spray bottle. The gentle spray is easier on young plants, and several light waterings are better than a gush of water, which can dislodge new roots. Some people prefer to place seedlings on a tray and water from below.

CARE AND FEEDING OF THE GARDEN

Well-prepared, fertile soil is vitally important for good plant growth. Growing naturally disease- and pest-resistant plants starts with building a soil that is alive and as healthy as possible.

SOIL COMPOSITION

"Soil" is a mixture of mineral particles of various sizes, organic material, water, and air. You can do an easy test to determine your soil type by rubbing some garden dirt between your fingers. Soils that are sandy feel gritty, and you can easily see the individual grains. Sandy soils contain many air spaces, are easy to dig, drain well, and warm up quickly in the spring; however, they may be quick to dry out. Crops grown in sandy soils require extra watering, which can leach valuable nutrients.

Heavy clay soils contain few air spaces and tend to pack together tightly; individual particles are too small to be seen, and the texture is sticky and slick. Clay soils tend to be fairly fertile but are hard to till, especially when damp. Although good at retaining moisture, clay soils with poor drainage can lead to waterlogged conditions and plant death.

SOIL PH ANALYSIS

The abbreviation *pH* refers to hydrogen-ion activity and is a measure of the acidity or alkalinity of your soil. The pH scale runs from 1 to 14, with a reading of 7 being neutral, neither an alkaline nor acid soil; numbers higher than 7 signify an alkaline soil, numbers lower than 7 signify an acid soil. Most vegetables do well in slightly acid to neutral soil because microorganisms that convert atmospheric nitrogen into a form that plants can use thrive best at 6.3 to 6.8. This pH range is also best for soil bacteria that decompose mulch and compost into humus. In this pH range, all the essential soil minerals that plants depend on for nutrients are maximally available. A simple soil test purchased at your local nursery will easily and accurately give you a soil pH reading.

LEAD CONTAMINATION

Lead is a toxic heavy metal. Consumption of even a little of it can cause severe and permanent damage, especially in young children. Lead is invisible, but if it is present in the soil it will find its way into every plant that grows there, including parts you harvest for food. Garden soil situated along a heavily trafficked street will have a higher lead content. The most dangerous soil is that within 100 feet of a street, and levels can be five times the normal rate near stop signs and places where cars are forced to idle.

The other common source of lead contamination in garden soil is from lead-based paint, a common component of exterior house paints until the Environmental Protection Agency banned its use in the 1950s. If you have a wooden house built before that time, you can assume that its adjacent soil—out to about 10 feet—has some lead contamination.

To test the lead level in your soil, inquire at a local EPA office, county extension service, or toxics lab and seek professional help to deal with the problem.

COMPOST AND MANURES

Manure, compost, and any other organic material adds humus to sandy soils, which acts like a sponge to hold water and nutrients within your plant's root zone. Conversely, organic material will loosen a clay soil that drains poorly by introducing fibrous matter that allows air to penetrate the heavy mass. Every gardener's dream is a good *loam*—a moisture-retentive soil that is well drained and contains plenty of organic material.

A deeply dug, well-amended fertile soil will support heavier planting and produce a greater yield of larger vegetables. Any soil, especially garden soil, is in a process of constant change. Each season a great deal of organic material is used up or carried away in the harvest and a constant replenishing is necessary to maintain good soil health. Regular applications of compost and manure go a long way to rebuild soil that has been gardened intensively.

Compost

Anything that was once alive makes good compost: leaves, coffee grounds, grass clippings, sawdust, kitchen food scraps. Avoid meat, fat, cooking oils, and grease, as they are slow to decompose and their odor will attract rodents. To *compost* simply means to hurry up the natural decomposition process so you can get the organic material into the garden quickly. Home-grown, organic, and free of toxic chemicals, compost has been called "black gold"—well worth digging for!

HOW TO BUILD A COMPOST PILE

There are many different styles of commercial compost bins available on the market, but it can be as simple as a 3-foot-by-3-foot bottomless box with wood or wire fencing sides. Build your pile with leaves, kitchen debris, sawdust, and the like, layered with manure, garden soil, and small twigs. Dampen the pile with the hose to thoroughly moisten all the ingredients and wait. The beneficial microbes present in the soil and/or manure will begin to break down the other material. You can hasten the process by periodically turning the whole mixture with a pitchfork to introduce oxygen to the pile, which will further fuel the decomposition process. Adding weeds, vegetable trimmings, and other garden debris to the compost pile throughout the growing season is an effective and efficient practice that will return your garden's goodness—to the garden.

Manure

This is organic material that has already been processed by the digestive tract of an animal. Nitrogen rich—not to mention pungent—fresh manure must be further composted or aged before it can be spread around existing plants or you will risk "burning" them. Manure gathered from a barn, pen, or rabbit cage can be either spread and allowed to age in the garden or composted in a pile as already described. If you have animals you would be wise not to overlook this free source of garden nutrients. Believe it or not, manure is perishable. Too much direct rainfall will leach the nitrogen content out of the manure and potentially contribute to groundwater contamination. Allowing it to dry out will lock up its goodness, making its value unavailable to plants. Fortunately for gardeners without the space or inclination toward animal husbandry, well-aged bagged manure can be purchased at most nurseries and immediately worked into the garden soil. *Note: Cat and dog manure should not be used in the garden because it may carry disease.*

Green manure

By cultivating a crop of quick-growing plants, you can produce a generous amount of organic material that you then plow back into the garden, where it enriches the soil as it decomposes. Rye grass, buckwheat, alfalfa, clover, and vetch are popular green manure crops. Organic farmers will routinely put a field in green manure to bolster the soil after producing a heavy-feeding crop like corn or broccoli. Home gardeners typically plant green manure crops in the cool weather on either side of the growing season. Check with local gardening experts who can advise you on the best green manure choice for your area.

EARTHWORMS

These valuable tenants in your garden's soil subsist on decaying organic matter. Aristotle referred to them as the "intestines of the world." Their constant tunneling loosens soil texture, and their digestive process results in the excretion of *castings*, a mixture of organic and inorganic material rich in humus, water-soluble, and an almost perfect plant fertilizer. This valuable process may be harnessed with the creation of a simple worm bin. Properly bedded, stocked with red wigglers, and fed a measured but steady diet of kitchen waste, the worm bin will become a veritable eating machine, turning garbage into rich plant food. In a mild climate, you can place your bin outdoors out of direct sun. Where temperatures are more extreme, both hot and cold, locate your bin out of the weather in a heated basement or garage. Clever commercial models are available that will fit on a covered porch, a spare closet, even right under the kitchen sink!

HOW TO MANAGE A WORM BIN

Your worm bin can be made of wood, metal, or plastic, although wooden boxes will wear out in just 2 to 3 years unless they are protected with a polyurethane varnish and allowed to dry out once in a while. Building two boxes and rotating their use will greatly extend the lifespan of a wooden bin. The container should be just 8 to 12 inches deep, as this is as deep as the worms will tunnel. A deeper container will only encourage the growth of smelly microorganisms, which live where there is little or no oxygen. Width-wise, your bin should have 1 square foot of surface for each pound of garbage you'll be adding per week.

Worm bedding not only provides a medium to hold moisture in the bin but also gives you material in which to bury garbage. Good bedding materials include shredded cardboard and paper, manure, and leaves that have been thoroughly dampened but are not so wet as to drip. Add dampened peat moss or cocoa coir to any other bedding to lighten the mix, making it easier for the worms to make their way around the bin. A handful of garden soil added to the bedding helps the worms' gizzards break down food. Powdered limestone and pulverized egg shells also add grit, reduce acidity, and provide calcium for worm reproduction. *Note: Slake or hydrated lime will kill your worms.*

Stock your worm bin with red wigglers (*Eisenia foetida*, also known as the "manure worm" or "red hybrid"), which are capable of consuming large quantities of garbage, reproduce quickly, and thrive in a worm bin environment. Red wigglers have alternating red and buff stripes. Adults are $1^1/_2$ to 3 inches long and can reproduce every 7 days. Red wigglers may be purchased year 'round at bait shops and some garden centers in the spring. Check resources online if you do not have a local source, or check with your gardening friends. Anyone with an active worm bin will have worms to share.

Feed kitchen scraps to the worm bin every day or let them accumulate and add once or twice a week. Dig a shallow hole and bury the waste with a covering of about 1 inch of bedding material. With each feeding rotate your digging site to different areas around the surface of the box to evenly distribute and encourage the worms to use the entire bin. Adding more food than your worms can digest will produce a sour smell as the food rots. The rule of thumb is 2 pounds of worms per 1 pound of garbage per feeding. Vegetable and fruit scraps, pasta, bread, tea leaves, and coffee grounds and filters are all acceptable worm food. Do not add meat scraps or fats; these will smell strongly and attract rodents.

With each feeding monitor the bedding's moisture level and sprinkle with water when necessary. As the worms eat the food and bedding, you will begin to see castings. When the level of castings is such that the bedding is becoming heavy or used up, harvest the vermicompost, a mixture of castings and old bedding material, for use in the garden. Move the old bedding to one side of the bin and fill the empty side with new bedding. Add food scraps to the new bedding; over the course of a few days the worms will move to that side. Remove the now mostly worm-free mature vermicompost. For quicker results, scoop some processed vermicompost into a shallow cardboard-lined tray; over the course of a few hours the worms will burrow down to escape the light. Gently brush the now-worm-free surface compost into a bucket until only a writhing mass of worms remains in the bottom of the tray. Transfer worms into fresh bedding.

Work the harvested worm castings and bedding material into your garden's root zone or layer it on the surface of the soil for a rich nutritious boost. Brew a liquid fertilizer by steeping castings in water and using the resulting tea to water your plants.

MULCHING

A layer of organic material, newspaper, stone, bark, or even plastic that blankets exposed garden soil will smother weeds as well as provide a physical barrier to evaporation, helping to conserve soil moisture. Mulch is more a technique than an actual garden ingredient but is often used as a noun, as in "I need to buy some mulch to spread in the garden." Organic mulches are sometimes referred to as *feeding mulches* because as the lower layers decompose they add fertility to the soil as well. Stone and plastic mulches are best at conserving moisture, and black plastic—although not the most attractive option—is often used to warm the soil and get a jump on the planting season.

SOIL NUTRIENTS

The three major nutrients that all plants need are nitrogen (N), phosphorus (P), and potassium (K). The numbers found on packaged fertilizers, organic and chemical alike, refer to the percentage of these nutrients, always in NPK order, present in the contents of the package. Thus 5-10-5 indicates a formula of 5 parts nitrogen, 10 parts phosphorus and 5 parts potassium.

1. *Nitrogen.* Plants use nitrogen to build healthy leaves and stems. A plant lacking nitrogen gets yellow leaves and grows slowly. Heavy-feeding plants, like corn and brassicas, use nitrogen quickly. Replace nitrogen by adding blood meal, fish meal, cottonseed meal, cover crops, and manure.

2. *Phosphorus.* Plants use phosphorus to grow healthy root systems and flowers. Unlike nitrogen, phosphorus remains in the soil a long time after it has been added. In addition to being richly present in compost, it's also found in wood ashes, soft and rock phosphates, bone meal, and cottonseed meal.

3. *Potassium.* Plants use potassium to strengthen their tissues, resist disease, and develop the chlorophyll that enables them to make food from sunshine. In addition to compost, it's found in wood ashes, granite dust, cottonseed meal, kelp, and greensand. Potassium is like nitrogen in that it is quickly lost to the soil and must be replenished.

AN ARGUMENT AGAINST THE USE OF CHEMICAL FERTILIZERS

▶ Plants don't distinguish between organic or inorganic nutrients, but their impact on soil health is critical.

▶ Chemicals are injurious to soil microbes that naturally produce plant food, creating a sterile environment that must constantly be artificially replenished.

▶ Water-soluble chemical fertilizers leach and contribute to ground-water contamination, and the quick burst of food they do provide does not last for the entire growing season.

▶ Most artificial fertilizers are petroleum based.

▶ Chemical fertilizers do not improve soil texture and water-holding capacity the way mulch, compost, manure, and cover crops do.

GARDEN COMPETITION

WEEDS

A well-nourished plant is a healthy defense against most garden pests. However, there is a limited amount of fertility in any garden. If your garden has one weed for every vegetable plant, then half of your soil's plant food is going to the weeds and half to your vegetable plants. That means your vegetable plants will be half as big and healthy and productive as they could be if there were no weeds. Although the reality may not be quite that simple, the bottom line is that weeds compete with the plants you are trying to grow for soil nutrients, water, and sun.

Thoroughly till the garden each spring before planting to get rid of weeds that may have overwintered or sprouted in cool spring weather, and continue to diligently weed during the growing season. Cultivate between rows with a rototiller or a hoe and weed by hand close to the plants. The best time to hand weed is right after a rain, when the ground is damp; roots seem to relax their hold on the soft ground, only to regain their grip when things get hot and dry.

HAND TOOLS

Although a larger garden may employ a rototiller or even a tractor to work the soil, hand tools are invaluable for working in tight quarters and around existing plants.

Spade—a shallow blunt-nosed shovel used to "plow" or turn over the soil.

Spading fork—a fork that looks like a pitchfork, but with wide tines, also used to plow the soil.

Hoe—a long- or short-handled tool used for chopping and breaking up dirt clods to create a fine, crumbly soil ready for planting. There are several styles of hoes with narrow or wide, fixed or oscillating blades. All must be sharpened to remain effective as weeding tools.

Rake—its rigid or flexible tines are used to smooth the seed bed, level the dirt, spread fertilizers, and pull any remaining clods or rocks out of the seedbed.

Trowel—the pro gardener's upgrade of a big spoon, used for close-in hand weeding or digging holes for transplants.

GARDEN PESTS LARGE AND SMALL

If you plant a crop and then find that something else ate it before you could, you won't be the first person it ever happened to. The number of possible plant diseases and plant-devouring insect species, to say nothing of fungi and garden-munching mammals, is legion. The organic gardener's best defense against bacterial and fungal problems is well-nourished soil and plenty of sunshine and water. Frequent your local nursery and get to know experienced gardeners in your area to learn from their expertise. Most likely they will be able to help diagnose ailing plants and mystery weeds and offer important advice for dealing with regional pests and gardening conditions specific to your area.

Problem mammals

If you grow it, they will come. Critters don't understand property rights, and many gardens are often and disastrously lost to predators unless the owner takes garden defense seriously. Identify the predator (or the one that got into your neighbor's garden) and act quickly to prevent the problem or risk losing the fruit (and vegetables) of your labors.

In some parts of the United States, where the natural predators of deer have been eliminated, deer overpopulation has become a serious problem. They have no fear of people or cars, and their competition with each other, combined with the rapid loss of their natural habitat to development, pressures them to boldly graze in suburban yards. Fencing stops them—if it's high enough. Bury the fencing a foot or so under the ground and it will also serve to keep out rabbits, cats, and poultry. Top the fencing with an electrified wire or two and you may keep out garden-bandit raccoons.

Gophers, moles, and voles all do a great deal of damage with their tunneling. Adding insult to injury, gophers will feed on roots (moles and voles are content to dine on grubs and earthworms). You can try fencing them out with underground barriers, but it can be difficult to get them on the right side—that is, the *outside* of the barrier. Old-timers plant castor beans to repel the diggers, but this is not a good solution in gardens with children or animals as even a single seed of this very toxic plant can kill. Other, far less dangerous but admittedly quirky controls include chewing-gum or instant grits placed at the tunnel opening. An organic, castor oil–based spray may prove the best option of all. To control rats and mice, keep a few hungry cats.

Dogs, scarecrows, a motion-triggered sprinkling device, rotten eggs, hot peppers, garlic, human hair, even urine are all time-tested tools for defending your turf against most garden predators.

Slugs, snails, and insects

These diminutive predators, although much smaller than those just mentioned (and, it could be argued, less sentient and crafty beings) nonetheless can still wreak great havoc on a garden. Slugs are snails with no shells; both are land-dwelling mollusks with a voracious appetite for the stalks and tender leaves of most garden plants. Being soft-bodied and very slimy, slugs and snails are most active in the damp weather of spring; controlling their numbers early in the year will go a long way toward reducing their impact throughout the rest of the season. Use diatomaceous earth, copper stripping, or iron phosphate-based organic baits to combat slugs and snails. A well-placed saucer of cheap beer will also lure them to their demise.

Various chewing and sucking insects capable of damaging plants, ruining a crop, and spreading disease may be controlled by planting marigolds, alliums, evening primrose, wild buckwheat, baby blue eyes, candytuft, bishop's flower, black-eyed Susan, strawflowers, nasturtiums, angelica, and yarrow to attract beneficial insects, or purchase ladybugs, predatory mites, praying mantises, beneficial nematodes, parasitic wasps, and other "good bugs." All are powerful and natural allies in the war against bad bugs. When all these practices, hand picking, and good garden hygiene are not enough, as a final resort you can try biodegradable, environmentally safe, and natural plant-based sprays. A conscientious organic gardener should also be willing to give up or "tithe" a minor percentage of their crop back to Mother Nature.

Crop rotation and management

Buy disease-resistant seed varieties whenever available. Rotate each vegetable's planting area around the garden every year to avoid a build-up of pests or disease spores. Don't let them just lie in wait to devour next year's crop. Move the target! Don't leave disease-infected plants in the garden or add them to the compost pile. Put them on a separate trash pile or burn them to avoid spreading soil-borne contagion.

PART TWO

GUIDE TO
VEGETABLES

THE ONION FAMILY

THE ONION FAMILY 51

Green Onions. 51

    Scallions 51

    Bunching onions 52

    Chives 52

    Garlic chives 53

    Leeks 53

Bulbing and Clove Type Onions 54

    Globe onions 54

    Garlic and elephant garlic 56

    Shallots 57

Other Onions 58

LEAVES 59
   Lettuce 60
   The Giant Cabbage/Mustard Family 62
      Cabbage 62
      Brussels sprouts 64
      Chinese cabbage 65
      Kale 66
      Mizuna 67
      Mustard 67
      Rocket/arugula 68
   Spinach and Other Rich Greens 68
      Corn salad 68
      Spinach 69
      Swiss chard 70
      Orach 70
      Purslane 71
   Other Leaves 71

STEMS AND FLOWERS 73
   Stems 73
      Asparagus 73
      Cardoon 75
      Florence fennel 76
      Kohlrabi 76
      Rhubarb 77
   Other, Lesser-Known "Stems" 78
      Broccoli raab 78
      Sea kale 78
      Celeriac 78
      True celery 79

Flowers 79

    Globe artichoke 79

    Broccoli 81

    Cauliflower 82

ROOTS 85

Starchy Roots 86

    Potatoes 86

    Sweet potato 89

    Other starchy roots 90

Nonstarchy Roots 91

    Beets 91

    Carrots 92

    Parsnips 93

    Radishes 94

    Turnips and rutabagas 97

    Other nonstarchy roots 98

GRASSES AND GRAINS 101

Wheat 101

    Backyard wheat 101

Corn 104

    Sweet corn 105

Other Grasses and Grains 110

    Grain amaranth 110

    Bamboo 111

    Buckwheat 112

    Oats 112

    Quinoa 113

LEGUMES 115
Peas 115
Beans 117
Other legumes 120

GOURDS 123
Cucumbers 124
Melons 125
Summer squashes 128
Winter squash and pumpkins 128
Exotic squashes 130
Craft gourds 131

THE NIGHTSHADE FAMILY 133
Eggplant 134
Okra 135
Peppers 137
Tomatoes 139
Other nightshade family vegetables 143

HERBS 145
Angelica 146
Balm, lemon 147
Basil 147
Bay 148
Bee balm 148
Borage 149
Burnet, salad 149
Catnip 150
Chamomile, German 150

Chamomile, Roman 150

Chervil 151

Chives 151

Cilantro 151

Comfrey 152

Dill 152

Fennel 153

Lavender 153

Lemon verbena 154

Lovage 154

Marigold, pot 154

Marjoram, sweet and Greek oregano 155

Mint 155

Parsley, curly and Italian 156

Rosemary 157

Sage 158

Sage, pineapple 158

Savory, summer 159

Savory, winter 159

Tarragon, French 160

Thyme, common and lemon 160

Watercress 161

Organizing a list of crops suitable for cultivation by the home gardener can be cumbersome and confusing, not to mention time-consuming. For our purposes—that is, producing and enjoying healthy, delicious food—we have grouped vegetables into the following useful categories: The Onion Family, Leaves, Stems and Flowers, Roots, Grasses and Grains, Legumes, Gourds, The Nightshade Family, and Herbs.

THE ONION FAMILY

Closely related to lilies, the onion family (*Allium*) offers rich variety and a broad spectrum of flavors, from the mild and tender leek to the fiery punch of garlic. Unlike fragrant garden lilies, Alliums are rich in sulphur, which gives them their vivid flavor and distinctive aroma.

GREEN ONIONS
Scallions

Scallions actually aren't a variety of onion, but an early stage in the onion life cycle; these "green onions" are most often the young greens of immature globe onions, harvested when thick as a pencil and at least 6 inches tall. If you want to harvest green onions all summer long, thickly plant onion seed or sets at intervals all spring and thin the young plants as they grow to establish final spacing.

Bunching onions

Bunching onions (*Allium fistulosum*) are perennials, and as such they should be located where they can remain undisturbed. In fact, it's possible to keep patches of bunching onions going for 10 to 20 years in a fertile soil. Start seed in early spring, sowing thickly in a block directly in the garden. Bunching onions never form a bulb; the white bottoms always stay thin and straight, topped by a shock of green chive-like foliage. Harvest lightly in the first year, allowing the remaining plants to go to seed and self-sow. Next spring they'll be the first edible to appear in your garden and may be harvested as needed, although they're at their best early in the year.

Chives

Chives (*Allium schoenoprasum*) are hardy perennials with deep green, hollow leaves that grow in a clump 8 to 12 inches tall. Their mild onion flavor heralds spring. The lovely purple globe-shaped flowers in early summer are slightly stronger in flavor and when separated into individual florets are tasty additions to salads and make a beautiful and edible garnish.

PLANTING: Little pots of chives are one of the earliest culinary herbs to show up at nurseries each spring; they can be set out in the garden when temperatures are still quite cold. Seeds may be sown ¼ inch deep in fertile soil in full sun once the weather has settled. Divide clumps every 2 to 3 years and reset into the garden at 12-inch spacing to increase your stock; chives make a lovely border to both herb and ornamental gardens.

HARVESTING: Chives are at their best throughout spring. Snip the thin, grass-like tops often to encourage tender regrowth, and remove faded flowers before they set seed to keep plants full and productive.

Garlic chives

Garlic chives (*Allium tuberosum*), also known as Chinese chives or Oriental chives, are a different species from regular chives but are used in the same way. They are quicker to mature than regular chives, have flat grassy leaves with a delicate garlic flavor, and bear starry white flowers. Garlic chives are less hardy than regular chives; a harsh winter may kill unprotected plants.

PLANTING: Garlic chive plants appear in nurseries once spring has warmed and can be transplanted into the garden at that time. The seed needs a warm start (70 to 80°F) and is usually started indoors in thickly sown flats; transplant into the garden in clumps, first trimming roots to ½ inch.

HARVESTING: Snip the fine grassy foliage of garlic chives throughout the summer, removing spent flowers to maintain production.

Leeks

Leeks (*Allium ampeloprasum* var. *porrum*) are grown for their delicate-tasting, white fleshy stem.

PLANTING: Prepare a well-dug, fertile soil in full sun. Transplants are easier to place than seeds and provide a jump on the growing season when started indoors 50 days before the frost-free date. Leeks require a long growing season, typically 105 to 130 days to maturity, depending on the variety. When setting the transplants into the garden, trim a few inches from the top of each plant and space plants about 2 inches apart in every direction. This will allow you to harvest the young leeks at a "scallion" stage while thinning to an eventual spacing of 6 inches apart.

Every few weeks, mound soil around the growing leeks to "blanch" the shaft for a sweet flavor and tender texture. For cleaner leeks at harvest, keep the soil below where the leaves begin to fan; some people recommend transplanting into a trench that can gradually be filled in during the growing season.

HARVESTING: Leeks do not store well once harvested. Where winter is reasonably mild, mature leeks can winter over in the garden where they can be picked as needed and add interest and beauty for many months.

BULBING AND CLOVE TYPE ONIONS
Globe onions

Globe onions (*Allium cepa*) start out as green onions and mature to big bulbous roots once their tops wither. Globe onions come in yellow, white, purple, red, Bermuda, and many other varieties. Different varieties do better in different parts of the country; it pays to ask at your local nursery what does well in your area. In general, white varieties are milder and make better green onions; they are also the kind you raise to get little "pickling" onions. Yellow varieties are the best for winter-keeping; red varieties, although sweetest of all, do not store well.

PLANTING: Globe onions may be started from seed or from sets (tiny onions). Seeds are by far the most economical and produce beautiful scallions, but sets give you a head start on the growing season and a quicker harvest. In the south, fall sowings will winter over and produce an early crop of scallions as well as larger bulbs the following summer. In the rest of the country, start seed indoors as much as six weeks before the ground can be worked, or direct seed in early spring. To plant sets, furrow a shallow trench and place sets, pointed end up, about 2 to 3 inches apart in every direction and cover to the neck with soil.

Onions are heavy feeders and dislike competition from other plants including weeds. Either sets or seed grow well in cool, wet spring weather; irrigate in a dry spring for the best results. Pulling scallions actually improves conditions for the remaining onions by loosening their soil as well as removing competition.

HARVESTING: Onion varieties and even individual plants differ widely in how quickly they grow. Planting from seed, you'll have green onions in 60 to 75 days; from sets, in about half that time. To grow large globe onions you'll need long, sunny days. The more top growth your onions make early in the season, the bigger the bulbs will be when those long, sunny days prompt the plants to begin transferring food from leaves to root.

Ideally, onions should be left in the ground until they mature and the tops dry up. If you are satisfied with the size of the bulbs, you can hurry the maturing process by twisting or knocking over the still-green tops. Wait a few days to pull or dig the bulbs. Spread the bulbs out on top of the ground or in a warm dry room until the tops are thoroughly dry. Bag and store in the dark. Use smaller onions first, as they do not keep as well as larger bulbs.

Garlic and elephant garlic

Garlic (*Allium sativum*) is a different species from elephant garlic (*Allium ampeloprasum*), but they are much alike in their cultivation and use. Both plants are perennial, and although elephant garlic is significantly hardier than regular, both can withstand frost and light freezing, making them a valuable overwintering crop in areas with moderate winters. Garlic has flat, grass-like leaves that grow 1 to 2 feet tall; elephant garlic plants are larger and require more garden space. Elephant garlic heads and cloves are also much larger than those of true garlic and are mild enough to be used raw in salads or substituted in any onion recipe, tasting like a garlic-flavored onion.

PLANTING: Garlics are propagated by deeply rooted bulbs or *heads* that grow underground. Each head is made up of a cluster of individual parts called *cloves*. The plants grow best during cool weather, developing strong top growth and the stored energy with which they will ultimately make cloves. Optimally, each plant will yield an average head of fifteen cloves. Planting in late August to mid-October allows the longest growing season; if you wait to plant in spring, do so as soon as the ground is no longer frozen. Some folks say you'll have good luck in the coming year if you plant your garlic on New Year's Day (weather permitting).

Prepare a fertile bed in full sun with a humus-rich, slightly acid soil. A loose, sandy soil allows the maturing bulbs to expand as they grow. Plant individual cloves, pointed end up, directly in the garden 2 to 3 inches deep and 3 inches apart in every direction and shallowly cover the points with soil. Keep plants weed free and well watered. Garlic repels many insects and is often planted with other vegetables and ornamentals.

HARVESTING: Stop watering when garlic leaves are a foot high (taller for elephant garlic). Like onions, garlic doesn't bulb up until the last 45 days of its growing season; to hurry them, knock over the above-ground shoots 90 to 110 days after planting. When the foliage has yellowed, loosen the dirt and pull up the whole plant. Don't cut off the leaves if you're planning to braid the garlic for storage. Brush soil from the bulb's outer skin and dry in the sun or in a warm room.

Shallots

Shallots (*Allium ascalonicum*) are a close relative of garlic, easy to grow and generously productive. Like garlic, they reproduce by bulb division underground. The "nest" of 3 to 10 or more shallot bulbs resembles a head of garlic, except that there are fewer cloves and no outer papery sheath.

PLANTING: Shallots are hardy, growing even in cold weather, and are not harmed by freezing. An early spring planting date is advised to give them the 100 days to maturity needed before bulb production shuts down with midsummer heat. In hot southern zones, plant shallots in the fall for a late winter or early spring crop.

Prepare a fertile, well-drained soil in full sun and shallowly plant individual bulbs, pointed end up, barely covering their necks with soil. Space plants 4 to 6 inches apart in every direction. Green shoots will grow to about 8 inches tall and can be sparingly harvested and used like a green onion.

HARVESTING: When leaves die back and yellow, gently lift the nest of bulbs from the soil and dry for 2 to 3 days. Store in an open-topped basket or braid like garlic and keep in a cool, dry location.

OTHER ONIONS

Various multiplying and top-setting onions are hardy perennials, providing a savory harvest year after year and requiring little effort or space. Multiplying onions (*Allium cepa* var. *aggregatum*), which include potato onions and Welsh onions, form a cluster of underground bulbs from a single planted bulb, increasing in number and size with every year. Topsetting onions (*Allium cepa* var. *proliferum*), also known as tree or walking onions, multiply their small underground bulbs each year as well as produce clusters of small ½-inch bulblets at the top of each seed stalk. These lesser-known novelties are fun to experiment with in the garden and well worth seeking out.

LEAVES

Basically, greens are edible-leaved plants. Sweet, rich, or pungent, fresh greens provide a rainbow of flavors, textures, and good eating. Some form or another can be harvested from the garden throughout the calendar year in most parts of the country.

Annual, biennial, or perennial, most greens are sown annually and harvested when young for their tasty and tender new leaves. Your climate and the time of year you want to harvest are factors in choosing what greens to plant. Most salad greens grow best in the cool moist temperatures of spring and fall, but it is possible to have salad year-round if you grow the right greens in the right way. Providing shade can mitigate hot summer temperatures, which tend to turn cool-season greens bitter and weak, but if you live where summers are very hot, planting chards, collards, and other heat-loving greens will produce better results.

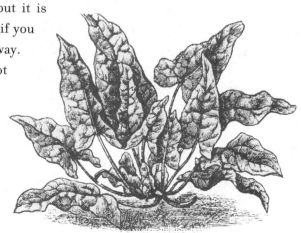

LETTUCE

Lettuce (*Latuca sativa*) is generally eaten fresh and the most common groups are as follows:

Butterhead lettuce makes a loose leafy head consisting of tender, buttery leaves with a garden-fresh flavor. They take a little longer to mature than leaf lettuce and can't stand hot weather. 50 to 65 days to maturity.

Crisphead lettuce is the hardest to grow in the home garden and takes twice as long to mature as leaf lettuce. The most familiar crisphead is the nostalgic iceberg lettuce with its mild (some would say bland) flavor and crisp, crunchy texture. Hot weather, especially hot nights, will turn crispheads bitter and cause them to prematurely go to seed. Space plants 8 to 18 inches apart, wider for bigger heads. 80 to 95 days to maturity.

Looseleaf lettuce is the easiest to grow, hardiest in hot weather, and the most nourishing. Leaf lettuce has a somewhat stronger flavor and its deeper green (or red or maroon or speckled) leaves have a higher nutrient content than butterhead or crisphead lettuces. 40 to 55 days to maturity.

Romaine lettuce, also called *cos*, grows straight up in a tight central bunch instead of curling into a ball or waving loosely. Romaine tolerates more heat than head or butterhead lettuce but not as much as leaf lettuce. Germination can be spotty, so sow thickly. Romaine varieties do best in damp, cool conditions. 70 to 85 days to maturity.

PLANTING: Prepare a fine, crumbly seedbed to accommodate lettuces' small and relatively weak root systems. Sow seed ¼ to ½ inch deep in early spring, as early as the ground can be worked; even young plants can withstand a light freeze. Leaf lettuce can be broadcast in a block for cut-and-come-again harvesting at a young stage, whereas head lettuces should be spaced 8 inches apart in every direction in rows or raised beds. The young thinnings of all lettuces are sweet and tender, so plant densely and thin in stages as the maturing plants need more room, tossing the young thinning into early salads.

Lettuce can be started indoors and transplanted into the garden at the four-leaf stage. Due to the extremely perishable nature of lettuce, both in the ground and once harvested, plan to succession plant every 2 to 3 weeks to ensure a continuing harvest. Provide regular water to prevent wilting and keep lettuce growing quickly. The long days of early summer trigger lettuce to bolt—that is, flower and go to seed.

HARVESTING: Whichever method you choose, pick lettuce in the cool of the day.

LETTUCE HARVEST METHODS

- ▶ Cut-and-come-again: Cut the whole plant about 2 or 3 inches above the ground and leave the remaining crown to regrow another crop.

- ▶ Harvest just the outer leaves, leaving the younger inner leaves to mature. Keep up with the maturing plants, as the outer leaves are the first to become bitter and tough.

- ▶ Harvest whole plants by thinning when young or at maturity.

THE GIANT CABBAGE/MUSTARD FAMILY

Crunchy, biting, colorful, hardy, toothsome, and sometimes stinky, cabbage and its close relatives the mustards contribute a piquant zest and nutritious wallop to salads, stir-fries, and casseroles. They are hearty greens eaten fresh when very young but are most often cooked.

Cabbage

Cabbage (*Brassica oleracea*) is relatively easy to grow, a heavy producer, and very nutritious; the American Cancer Society advises us to eat cabbage (and other cruciferous, sulfur-containing vegetables) to protect against cancer. There are cabbage varieties with all kinds of maturing dates and sizes—from little heads about the size of a football that mature in 60 days to giant kinds that make 50-pound heads over a long season. Heads may be tightly formed or loose; loose-leafed savoy cabbage is particularly hardy and very tasty, an excellent choice for home gardeners. Color choices include pink, red, lavender, blue, purple, white, cream, or green, making for an ornamental as well as nourishing crop.

PLANTING: Provide fertile soil in full sun and plant seed ¼ to ½ inch deep and 3 inches apart, or set transplants into the garden, spacing the plants 2 to 3 feet apart in every direction. In the North, start transplants of early spring cabbage in a hotbed or indoors in February, setting plants into the open garden as soon as the ground is workable. In the South, start early spring cabbage in the fall and transplant into the garden in January. For an extended harvest, plant a combination of early-, midseason-, and late-maturing cabbages. 65 to 85 days to maturity.

HARVESTING: Early cabbage matures quickly and may split if left too long, while mid- and late-season cabbages, which mature in late summer and fall as the weather is cooling, will hold for much longer in the garden without splitting. Cut close to the head, leaving the stem, and continue to water to get a second crop of smaller heads each about the size of a baseball. Cabbage can stand nighttime temperatures down to 20°F, making it a good candidate to overwinter in the garden.

BANISH BUGS WITH HERBS

Scatter dill seed among young cabbages or plant a row of thyme alongside to repel insects. A mixture of boiled onion and garlic sprayed on the plants will also deter bugs. To control root maggots, spread wood ashes around each plant, digging some into the ground at the roots; replace the ash after heavy rains until maggot season is over at the end of June.

Brussels sprouts

Brussels sprouts (*Brassica oleracea gemmifera*) are curious plants that grow 2 to 4 feet tall and are available in green or purple varieties. What are essentially little cabbage-type heads grow all around a stout stem that is crowned with a shock of leaves, making the plant look like a mini palm tree. Brussels sprouts are sweetest after they've been through several light frosts and are generally planted to mature throughout fall and winter.

PLANTING: In an area of full sun, prepare a very fertile soil to sustain the plants over their very long growing and harvest season. Sow seed ¼ to ½ inch deep and 3 inches apart directly into the garden in late spring. Transplants may be started indoors 6 to 8 weeks before setting out in the garden. Thin or space plants 14 to 18 inches apart in rows that are 30 inches apart. 65 to 110 days to maturity.

HARVESTING: Sprouts grow close-packed on the plant's main stem at the base of each leaf, maturing from the bottom of the stem up. Temperate-zone plants may produce until Thanksgiving; in milder climates they can be harvested all winter. Harvest the lowest sprouts when they are just ½ inch wide on up to full-sized at 1 to 1½ inches across by gently twisting the sprout free from the stem; larger sprouts become yellow and tough. Be careful not to damage the plant, and 2 or 3 smaller sprouts may regrow where you picked the first. Once harvesting begins, snap off the leaves halfway up the plant, beginning at the bottom, to encourage the plant to grow taller and more productive.

Chinese cabbage

Chinese cabbage (*Brassica rapa*) is more closely related to mustard than to cabbage. The varieties are grown, stored, and prepared much like cabbage. Chinese cabbage has a milder taste and more delicate texture and is more digestible than regular cabbage, a fact appreciated by many people. Chinese cabbage may be divided into heading and nonheading types: Chinese celery cabbage, nappa cabbage, and *wong bok* are heading varieties; nonheading varieties include bok choy, Chinese mustard cabbage, and pak choi, which are similar to Swiss chard, with loosely bunching green leaves and a thick midrib.

PLANTING: Prepare a light, well-drained soil and sow seed ¼ to ½ inch deep and 2 inches apart in rows that are 30 inches apart. Thin when plants are 3 inches high, 4 weeks old, or have 5 true leaves. Thin nonheading types to 9 inches, heading types to 12 to 15 inches apart. Plants must never dry out during the growing season and are best irrigated at ground level to discourage disease and rot.

Spring crops do better where summers are cool, with transplants started indoors 8 to 10 weeks before the last frost date and set out 1 month later; growth will be stunted and the plants will likely bolt if transplanted after 1 month. Chinese cabbage grows best when days are becoming shorter and temperatures are cooling. Plants are hardy to 20°F, and many gardeners skip the spring crop and instead plant in late July or early August (about 12 weeks before first frost date) for a fall harvest that will hold in the garden long into winter. 70 to 85 days to maturity.

HARVESTING: You can harvest Chinese cabbage at any age; however, some varieties taste best after frost. Pull the entire plant to harvest heading types; do the same for nonheading varieties or just remove the outer leaves, leaving at least 5 leaves at the center of the plant to size up and mature.

Kale

Kale (*Brassica oleracea* var. *acephala*) handles cold and heat quite well and can be raised from the Deep South to Alaska. These resemble a frilly, headless cabbage that you harvest leaf by leaf. It's likely to be the hardiest vegetable you've ever raised and will withstand even Midwestern winters, sweetening in flavor with cold temperatures. Russian kale (*B. oleracea* var. *fimbriata*), actually a cousin to the rutabaga, has looser, often reddish-tinted leaves. Russian kale prefers to be directly sown in the garden and although less winter hardy is sweeter in warm weather. Collards (*B. oleracea* var. *acephala*), a form of kale, are a traditional southern food and nearly the only brassica that thrives in the South, where they are easy to grow and disease-free.

PLANTING: In the South collards and kale are planted from July to November for harvest during the fall and winter. Transplants can be started indoors in late winter, to be set out as soon as the ground can be worked in spring for an early crop before summer heat sets in. Many northern gardeners don't bother planting kale in the spring, preferring to use the space to grow early peas or lettuces. Once those crops are harvested, a mid-summer planting of kale, as much as 40 days before your frost-free date, will yield plants that produce over the fall and winter.

Sow seed directly in the garden ½ inch deep and 1 inch apart; thin young plants to 6 to 12 inches apart, working up to 18- to 24-inch spacing for mature plants. Begin transplants indoors 5 to 7 weeks before setting out into the garden. Adequate summer water is necessary for plants to withstand heat. Days to maturity: kale 55 to 70; collards 85.

HARVESTING: You can harvest individual leaves as you need them, leaving the plants to generously produce more. Very cold weather will slow growth and cause the outer leaves to toughen, but they will protect the tender inner leaves. Kale will start to grow again in the spring, offering a final harvest before flowering and going to seed.

Mizuna

Mizuna (*Brassica rapa* var. *japonica*), also known as *kyona*, is a relatively mild-flavored mustard green with attractive, feathery foliage that is not usually bothered by pests. (*See Rocket/arugula entry for planting and harvesting information.*)

Mustard

Mustard (*Brassica juncea*), also called mustard greens or mustard spinach, is stronger in taste and tougher in texture than spinach and chard with a biting hot flavor that is less pronounced when grown in cool weather. (*See Rocket/arugula entry for planting and harvesting information.*)

Rocket/arugula

Rocket/arugula (*Eruca sativa*), also called garden rocket and Mediterranean salad, can and will germinate in the very wettest, coldest spring soils. Rocket seems to pop out of the ground and up in a flash, just like its name.

PLANTING: Prepare a fertile soil and sow seed directly in the garden ¼ to ½ inch deep as early as February or March; rocket is a particularly good candidate for broadcast sowing for an early cut-and-come-again harvest. Seeds of these spicy greens will germinate rapidly and mature in 35 to 45 days. For a steady supply of the most tender leaves, it's best if you plant a few seeds every week and keep picking for a constant supply of flavorful, young plants. These cool-season greens are all prone to spring bolting and turn tough and bitter in warm weather. Allow plants to self sow or replant seed in fall for a second growing season.

HARVESTING: Cut when the leaves are 4 to 6 inches long, as larger leaves toughen and become spicy-hot. The plants will bolt as soon as long days trigger them to do so. Fall-planted mustard greens will stand through light frosts and improve in flavor.

SPINACH AND OTHER RICH GREENS
Corn salad

Corn salad (*Valerianella locusta*)—also called lamb's lettuce, *fetticus*, and *mache*—is a small, flat, ground-hugging plant with oval or round leaves that have a very mild, sweet flavor. Corn salad is a special treasure in the winter, as it is one of the few delicate-tasting greens you can harvest from your garden between late December and April.

PLANTING: Sow ½ inch deep, plant generously to allow for what can be spotty germination, and thin to 3 or 4 inches between plants. If you live in a cool-summer area, you can succession-plant from spring through fall. In a hot-summer area, you can manage a summer crop by planting corn salad where it will receive afternoon shade, or plant August through September for a fall crop. Seed broadcast over the bare garden when you are doing fall cleanup will germinate with the fall rains, winter in a small rosette, and finish growing in spring. 40 to 50 days to maturity or fall sown for a spring crop.

HARVESTING: Pick (don't cut) individual leaves as they size up, or harvest an entire plant at once. Handle the leaves gently so as not to bruise them, and they will keep for a week in the refrigerator.

Spinach

Spinach (*Spinacia oleracea*) is one of the earliest spring green crops in the garden. Its delicious, mild leaves are rich in vitamins and minerals and ready for harvest weeks before chard. However, with long days and warm, dry conditions spinach quickly bolts and goes to seed, putting an abrupt end to its harvest.

PLANTING: Plant seed ¼ inch deep directly in the garden, thinning to an eventual 12-inch spacing between individual plants. Spinach can be slow to germinate, so a sprinkling of fast-sprouting radish seed will help to mark the planting area. Where spring quickly gives way to warm weather, plant spinach in partial shade to help prolong the harvest. 65 days to maturity.

HARVESTING: Clip using a cut-and-come-again method, harvesting individual leaves from the outside of plants, allowing the inner leaves to continue to develop.

Swiss chard

Swiss chard (*Beta vulgaris cicla*) is botanically a beet with an undeveloped root and delicious leaves. The remarkably beautiful Rainbow chard has become an ornamental favorite as well as a vegetable garden staple. Gardeners in the hot interior United States favor it in the summer garden because it doesn't bolt the way spinach does. You can also plant it early because it is as hardy against spring frosts as it is against summer heat. Maritime gardeners plant a second crop in July for harvest beginning in the fall and going on through winter.

PLANTING: Prepare a fertile soil to sustain a long harvest and plant as you would beets. 50 to 60 days to maturity.

HARVESTING: Pick individual leaves 1 inch above the root level. Water well and the plants will quickly recover to produce another crop—and another!

Orach

Orach (*Atriplex hortensis*), also known as mountain spinach or giant lamb's-quarters, does well in regions where spring is too short to cultivate other mild-flavored greens and thus is a good substitute for common spinach.

PLANTING: Sow seed ¼ inch deep and thin plants 8 to 12 inches apart. Orach is tolerant of poor soil conditions. Left alone, orach can grow to 6 feet, with a plume-like flower followed by a fabulous seedhead that will self-sow thickly if allowed to mature. 42 to 55 days to maturity.

HARVESTING: Pick or cut young plants when they are 4 to 6 inches, or harvest the tender top growth on taller plants as the lower leaves toughen.

Purslane

Purslane (*Portulaca oleracea*) is a low-growing perennial that can thrive in any soil. It needs moisture to germinate and get going but can handle very dry conditions once established. Use leaves and stems in salad or cook like spinach. The flavor is tart, and the plant is rich in vitamin C and omega-3 fatty acids that help prevent heart and circulatory problems.

OTHER LEAVES

Bitter greens like endive, radicchio, and escarole; wild collected greens like nettles, sorrel, dandelions; and the leafy parts of other vegetables like beets and turnips are all possible choices for producing healthy, home-grown greens.

STEMS AND FLOWERS

We don't think of them as stems or flowers per se, but the following vegetables are all either the new shoot of an emerging plant, the edible stem or a food-storing root-like bulge in the stem, or the flowering bud of a plant. These fleshy parts function as the plant's food storage site and as such are filled with nutrients, not to mention flavor.

STEMS

Asparagus

Asparagus (*Asparagus officinalis*) is a long-lived perennial. It does well in areas with cool growing seasons and winters that are cold enough to provide a dormant season. It is one of the very earliest and most delectable crops to harvest in the spring garden; however, it can take up a lot of space and be both difficult to grow and slow to start producing. For that reason most gardeners plant established roots or "crowns" rather than starting from seed,

which adds considerably to the years before harvest. Asparagus plants are either male or female. Female plants may be identified by the (poisonous) red berries amongst the fern-like growth in summer. Purchase crowns labeled "all-male," as these are considered to be more productive, with fatter spears.

PLANTING: When siting your asparagus bed, keep in mind that the plants can live and produce for as long as 20 to 25 years. If space allows, establish a long row along the outside edge of your vegetable garden. This will allow the plants to remain undisturbed by cultivation, yet easily accessible for care and harvest; otherwise plant in widely spaced rows as in the guidelines that follow. Plant crowns in the early spring in the North. In the South, a fall planting is recommended to take advantage of several months of cooler weather before the onset of summer heat.

Mature, productive asparagus plants have strong root systems that spread as much as 6 feet wide and reach 6 to 8 feet deep. A deeply dug, well-drained, rich soil will help plants establish quickly. Prepare a trench 18 inches deep in rows 4 feet apart. Cover the bottom of the trench with a 6-inch layer of well-rotted manure topped with 6 inches of topsoil. Set asparagus crowns 12 to 18 inches apart at the bottom of the trench and cover them with 2 inches of soil. As the plants grow, gradually cover them with more soil from the sides of the trench. Both new and established asparagus beds benefit from 4 to 6 inches of manure or compost each spring and again in the fall to retain moisture, keep weeds down, and provide the heavy feeding the plants require.

HARVESTING: Wait to harvest until plants are established, according to the age of the crowns purchased—1 year for 3-year-old crowns, as much as 3 years for 1-year-old crowns. Mature plants will yield a harvest for a period of 6 to 8 weeks, beginning in spring and ending in early summer. When spears are 4 to 6 inches tall, cut or snap off by hand at ground level or just below. Young tender spears will have tightly closed tips and a ready snap to their stems; larger spears become tough and stringy. Continue to harvest regularly to keep the plants producing. Once the harvest period is over, allow the spears to mature into tall, fern-like fronds that will gather and store energy for production of the next year's crop. Wait to cut down the foliage until it has completely yellowed in the fall.

Cardoon

Cardoon (*Cynara cardunculus*) is a tender perennial of the thistle family closely related to the globe artichoke and similar in flavor. Although its huge leaf stalks have been cultivated for over 30,000 years around the Mediterranean, it is little known and seldom grown in the United States.

PLANTING: In the North, sow seed indoors in March and move transplants into the garden in a sunny position after last frost. In the South, cardoons can be sown directly into the garden in the spring. Cardoons get big! These dramatic and architectural plants can make quite an ornamental impact in the garden, but they must have space; allow 6 feet between plants. Mature cardoon stalks are tough and virtually inedible for their bitterness; blanching, a process of starving the plant of light, sweetens the stalks and removes their harsh flavor. Transplant or sow seed in trenches, gradually filling with soil as the plants mature to produce tender, edible cardoon hearts. 60 to 85 days to maturity.

HARVESTING: Gather the young stalks and their mild, pale, meaty leaf-ribs from the center of the plant, cutting them off near the root and discarding the tough outer stalks. In a mild climate where winter temperatures do not fall below the high 20s you can divide your harvest between fall and spring.

Florence fennel

Florence fennel (*Foeniculum vulgare*), sweet fennel, or *finnochio* is grown for the swollen stems that develop at the base of the plant. These white bulbous portions of the stems have a crunchy texture and a mild licorice-celery flavor when fresh, becoming even sweeter and more tender when cooked.

PLANTING: Prepare a light, fertile soil in full sun. Sow seed directly into the garden between April and mid-July, as plants do not transplant well; in warm climates plan for a later sowing so the crop will mature in cool weather. Gradually thin to a foot apart, harvesting the young thinnings for salads. As Florence fennel matures, mound soil over the base of each plant to blanch and sweeten the developing bulb. 90 days to maturity.

HARVESTING: Dig or pull to harvest when the bulb is 2½ to 3 inches wide; larger bulbs become tough and stringy. The plants will tolerate light frosts.

Kohlrabi

Kohlrabi (*Brassica oleracea* var. *gongylodes*) is a fast-maturing, pest- and disease-free brassica whose edible part tastes like an apple and looks like an above-ground turnip (a close relative). Available in green or purple varieties, plants form curious bulbous stems at soil level topped with a frilly crown of leaves.

PLANTING: Prepare a fine, fertile, sandy seedbed in full sun and sow seed ¼ to ½ inch deep, thinning to 3 to 6 inches between plants with 12 to 24 inches between rows. Kohlrabi is tolerant of both cold and heat and can be directly sown in the garden. Spring plantings are best sown in small successions beginning 4 to 6 weeks before the frost-free day to allow for several subsequent crops to be harvested before warm weather turns the kohlrabi flesh woody and unpleasantly hot. Fall crops may be sown beginning in late July and will hold for harvest in cooling temperatures without losing their sweetness. Keep the plants well watered and free from the competition of weeds. 45 to 60 days to maturity.

HARVESTING: Harvest spring-planted kohlrabi when only 1 to 2 inches in diameter for optimum flavor and tenderness. Maturing in cool fall weather, later crops can grow to 3 to 4 inches in diameter and maintain quality, keeping well in the garden and withstanding temperatures even down into the 20s.

Rhubarb

Rhubarb (*Rheum rhabarbarum*) is a long-lived, hardy perennial from Siberia. A good plant for the northern third of the United States, rhubarb actually thrives on being frozen all winter and is one of spring's earliest producers.

PLANTING: Plant 2- or 3-year-old roots in fertile soil in spring or fall in an area of other permanent plantings; the beautifully ornamental leaves make this plant a good candidate for working into the perennial border. Well fed, mature plants grow 2 to 3 feet tall and as wide; space accordingly. Remove flower spikes as they appear to maintain peak production of edible stalks.

HARVESTING: Allowing a year for the plants to establish, you can begin to harvest lightly by cutting or twisting and pulling the largest individual stalks. In subsequent years as much as ⅔ of the stalks may be pulled, leaving the remaining ⅓ to replenish the roots for the next year's crop. *Note: Rhubarb leaves contain toxic oxalic acid; discard or use to mulch around the plants.*

OTHER, LESSER-KNOWN "STEMS"

Broccoli raab

Broccoli raab (*Brassica rapa* var. *ruvo*), also called *rapini*, is an Italian vegetable that's eaten leaves, buds, flowers, and all. It's kind of a loose-topped broccoli or, more precisely, the flowering stem of a turnip. Easier to grow than broccoli, it's a gardener's veggie you don't see in stores. Use planting directions for kohlrabi to produce spring and fall crops and harvest when flower stalks have developed buds but are not yet open. 35 to 50 days to maturity.

Sea kale

Sea kale (*Crambe maritima*) is a European perennial cultivated at least since the Romans. Sea kale does best in cool seashore regions. Like rhubarb, it is an early crop and beautiful enough to include in ornamental perennial plantings. In early spring, before new growth has commenced, place a bucket over the plant's crown to blanch the new growth; this removes their inherent bitterness. Harvest shoots that are 4 to 12 inches tall, continuing until leaves begin to unfurl in late spring. Remove the bucket and nurture the plant through the growing season to rebuild its energy stores.

Celeriac

Celeriac (*Apium graveolens* var. *rapaceum*), a little-known relative of celery, is a valued winter veggie in Europe. Other names for it are celery root, knob celery, and turnip-rooted celery. The edible part is its enlarged, knobby combination stem base-root crown-tap root. Cultivation is similar to kohlrabi. 110 days to maturity.

True celery

True celery (*Apium graveolens* var. *dulce*) is a slow and challenging crop in the home garden. However, garden-fresh celery is delicious, and—if you have rich soil and live where summers are cool—worth a try. Leaf celery (*Apium graveolens secalinum*) or cutting celery is a good substitute; the thin leafy stalks are too strong to eat fresh, but are a good flavoring herb in the kitchen. 100 to 120 days to maturity.

FLOWERS

Globe artichoke

Globe artichoke (*Cynara scolymus*) is a semihardy thistle variety that thrives in southern coastal areas with a mild weather climate year 'round. Artichokes are short-lived perennials with an average lifespan of 5 years. A well-fed, mature artichoke plant may grow to 5 feet by 5 feet and represents an extravagant use of garden space, but it's a delicious choice if you've got the right conditions. Newer varieties have been developed that, although much smaller, are quick to mature, allowing gardeners in colder areas to grow them as annuals.

PLANTING: Like asparagus, globe artichokes are heavy feeders that require a well-drained, sandy soil rich in humus and thrive with annual applications of manure or compost. Purchase young plants at the nursery or remove a 12-inch side shoot or sucker from a mature plant, being sure to include some roots with your cutting. Place plants or suckers 24 inches apart, hilled like squash, in rows 3 feet apart.

HARVESTING: Each plant will produce from 2 to 20 artichokes per season. A mature artichoke resembles a large scaly head, similar to a pine cone, growing at the top of a long stalk. Harvest the heads by cutting 1 to 2 inches below the bud before it has begun to open; if in doubt, cut too young, as once the buds begin to flower they will turn woody and inedible. When artichokes are very young and tender, the flower bulbs and even the peeled stems may be eaten fresh. Once matured and hardened, artichokes must be steamed or boiled to render the meaty base of each immature petal (bract) of the unopened flower bud and the inner heart tender and edible.

Continue to harvest faithfully throughout the season, although those buds that mature in the hottest part of the summer are tougher than those that come before or after the heat. One advantage to growing your own crop is the ability to harvest the chokes when only the size of an egg and before the flowers have developed their thistly centers. These young buds, not generally available in groceries, can be simply sliced and sautéed.

Broccoli

Broccoli (*Brassica oleracea* var. *botrytis*) has been grown in the Mediterranean and the Middle East for at least the last 2,000 years. The part we eat is the flower head, a mass of tiny unopened buds, and its stem. Broccoli varieties include green, purple (although it turns green when cooked), and white, as well as those that mature at different times of the year with large, small, or oddly shaped heads.

PLANTING: Broccoli likes lots of sun and not much heat, growing best in areas that have cool summers, cultivated as a spring or fall crop in hotter regions. It requires a sweet, fertile soil and regular water during the growing season. Somewhat subject to pests and disease, broccoli should not be grown in the same place year after year.

Purchase young plants or set out home-grown transplants in midspring when daytime temperatures average around 50°F. Space plants 18 to 24 inches apart in every direction or in rows 2 to 3 feet apart. You'll gain a few weeks of cool-season growing time with the use of a hot cap or cloche for weather protection.

For a fall crop, start seed directly in the garden 10 to 12 weeks before the first fall frost date. Sow seed ½ inch deep and 3 to 4 inches apart, allowing 7 to 10 days for germination. Thin to plant spacing as for spring. Weather permitting, hardy varieties may be sown in late summer to overwinter and produce shoots the

following spring; these are often referred to as "sprouting" broccoli. 45 to 85 days to maturity depending on variety.

HARVESTING: The first cluster or head the plant produces will be the
biggest; harvest this and all subsequent smaller clusters with a por-
tion of stem attached before the tightly closed buds begin to loosen
and flower. A few days after the central sprout is cut, the plant begins
to grow smaller side sprouts where leaves join the stem. Keep plants
well watered and side-dress with fertilizer to maximize this second
and all subsequent crops, continuing to harvest when clusters are
in the tight-bud stage. The plants will continue to produce until
first frost if you can prevent any flowers from blossoming.

Cauliflower

Cauliflower (*Brassica oleracea* var. *botrytis*) is best suited to a long, cool
and moist growing season and can be difficult to cultivate in other conditions. Varieties are available with white, green, purple, or even orange
heads that are rich in vitamins and nutrients.

PLANTING: Prepare a rich, well-dug soil in partial shade, as too
much heat causes the plant to head prematurely. Experimenters
have grown cauliflower with as little as 2 hours of sunlight each
day. Plant seed ¼ to ½ inch deep, 3 inches apart. Cauliflower seed
requires heat for germination, around 80°F. Grow transplants for
5 to 7 weeks before setting into the garden as soon as the soil can
be worked, setting plants 20 inches apart. Sow seed directly in the
garden in summer to take advantage of heat for germination, with
fall's shorter days and cooling weather promoting good growth.
Water regularly and mulch to maintain an even soil moisture and
combat weeds. 60 to 100 days to maturity depending on variety.

HARVESTING: Cauliflowers size up quickly once the heads begin to form. Harvest when they reach 6 inches in diameter or before the flower buds loosen and open. Each plant produces a single head. For particularly pure white curds, blanch when they are 3 to 5 inches in diameter by pulling up the large outer leaves over the head and securing with a rubber band or string. Wait for 4 to 12 days to harvest. Plants will hold well in the garden in cool weather and withstand light frosts.

ROOTS

Whether they are a true root, a tuber, or a corm—a rounded, thickened underground stem base—root vegetables are typically biennial plants that form a food storage part the first year and draw on that reserve in the second year to produce flowers and seeds. They may be divided into starchy and nonstarchy categories. Starchy roots, which tend to be a dietary mainstay wherever they're grown, include the potato and sweet potato as well as the lesser-known cassava, kudzu, malanga, taro, and yam. Nonstarchy roots, which are prepared fresh or cooked, include the beet, carrot, radish, turnip, and many more.

When planning to grow a root vegetable crop, prepare a well-tilled soil dug to the depth to which you expect that particular root to grow. A light, sandy loam, free of rocks and clods, with a steady supply of moisture will produce nice plump, straight roots that are easy to harvest and prepare.

STARCHY ROOTS

Potatoes

Potatoes (*Solanum tuberosum*) are easily grown in the home garden. Technically the potato is a member of the Nightshade family, along with tomatoes, peppers, and eggplant, but it appears in this chapter because potatoes are grown for their edible tubers or "roots"; indeed, all other parts of a potato plant are toxic.

Potato varieties include yellow, rose, blue skin/white flesh, blue skin/blue flesh, white, russet, red, black, purple, red skin/red flesh, red skin/gold flesh, color-splashed (multicolored), scab-resistant, best keeper, heirloom, and more. You can also choose from varieties that mature in early, mid, and late season, and between quicker- and slower-maturing varieties. 75 to 130 days to maturity.

PLANTING: Potatoes grow best in fairly cool weather with long days. They are impervious to light frosts and may be planted very early in the spring, 3 to 4 weeks before the expected last frost. Successive plantings may be made every few weeks until early summer for a continuous harvest. In warmth and humidity potatoes are subject to rot; southern gardeners should either choose a variety that is heat-resistant or plant in winter for a spring harvest before the hot days arrive.

Potatoes prefer an acid soil, so do not apply lime to the planting area. Prepare a well-dug soil with lots of organic matter and plant seed potatoes 3 to 6 inches deep every 6 to 8 inches in rows 2½ feet apart. Plant with the eye pointing up; sprouts will be up in 3 to 4 weeks. Keep beds well watered and free of weeds.

Straw bed planting is a method that simplifies planting and harvest but somewhat reduces your yield. Place seed potatoes on top of the soil, top with a foot of straw mulch, and water well.

Make sure the developing potatoes are kept well covered with straw throughout the growing season. At harvest time, rake back the straw and pick your crop.

HARVESTING: You can harvest baby potatoes before the main crop by gently digging near the surface under the soil or straw mulch to unearth the small tubers. Resettle the soil around the plant to allow the remaining tubers to keep growing. About 3 months after planting the potato plants will begin to yellow and whither. At this point the potatoes have stopped growing and are ready to dig. In hot weather they keep better in the ground; just dig as needed. After the weather cools the entire crop can be dug up, plant by plant, carefully sifting the roots and soil to get all the tubers. Cure the potatoes for storage by spreading them out in a warm dry place out of the sun for a week or two to allow small surface cuts to heal and the skins to thicken. *Note: Don't leave potatoes lying in the sunlight. They will develop a greenish tinge that not only tastes bad but is poisonous as well.*

SEED POTATOES

Seed potatoes are full-sized potatoes that are cut into pieces, cured, and planted. Each piece must be big enough to supply nourishment to the new plant until it sprouts and is capable of producing its own energy, and it must include at least one "eye"—a small round depression on the potato surface. An average potato will yield 3 to 5 seed pieces. Cure the cut pieces by allowing them to dry in a warm dry room for a couple of days to form a protective callus, which will guard against rot until the plants sprout. *Sets* are tiny potatoes that are planted whole and thus avoid the vulnerability of cut surfaces.

Regular store potatoes don't make the best seed potatoes; they are seldom labeled by variety, and they may have been sprayed with chemicals to inhibit sprouting. Purchasing your seed stock through a mail-order specialist or the local nursery in early spring not only assures you of accurate growing information but also offers you a broader choice of varieties to choose from.

Sweet potato

Sweet potato (*Ipomoea batatas*) is a tropical starchy root from the ancient Americas that although grown like a potato is not related. Sweet potatoes are one of the most nutritious foods from the garden, containing large amounts of vitamin A and beta carotene, but they need hot weather and a long growing season to produce. If your July through August mean temperature is more than 80°F, you're in an ideal zone for sweet potatoes. Less-than-ideal conditions will result in a reduced yield, but sweet potatoes can be grown as far north as southern New York, Michigan, and the Midwest.

PLANTING: Sweet potatoes require a long hot growing season and a well-cultivated soil that's not too rich; excess nitrogen will send growth to the vine instead of the root. Purchase starts or grow your own slips (see sidebar) and set plants every 1 to 3 feet, depending on variety, in rows 2½ feet apart. If you're short of garden space, run the 4- to 16-foot-long morning glory–type vines up a garden fence, or grow in a deep window box with the vines trailing down. Vines that spread out on the ground will root along their length; be careful to not damage these secondary roots, as that will decrease yield. Once established, plants can handle a dry spell without harm; they may even be stimulated to produce a better crop as a result.

HARVESTING: For all their long growing season, sweet potato roots put on the most growth during the end of their season—September and October. Planting too late or harvesting too early will yield undersized, low-starch roots that will fail to cure properly for storage. Wait as long as your season will allow and harvest sweet potatoes on a sunny, dry day when the soil is not wet. Dig with a fork very carefully to avoid damaging the crop. Spread the roots out on the ground in the sun for 2 to 3 hours to thoroughly dry.

In the South, where temperatures are 80 to 90°F, sweet potatoes can remain curing in the sun for another 10 to 14 days. In cooler climates they must be moved indoors to a very warm area for this curing period. Unlike most vegetables, sweet potatoes need damp conditions to cure; if the weather isn't humid, cover them with a slightly damp towel.

GROWING SWEET POTATO SLIPS

The sweet potato, like the white potato, is not grown from seed but is propagated from the root itself. The potato is a tuber with eyes that sprout, but the sweet potato is a true root with no eyes or buds. To produce sweet potato slips, about 5 to 6 weeks before garden planting time pot a sweet potato into a hotbed or container of soil at least 1 foot deep, burying the root halfway; smaller roots produce more slips. You can also lay the root in a pan of water to promote sprouting. Whichever method you choose, the temperature must be constantly warm, at least 75°F, and conditions moist.

When a sprout or slip is about 6 to 10 inches long and has produced roots, it's time to carefully separate it from the original root. Hold the parent plant tightly with one hand and pull to remove the offspring with the other. For extra growing time, transplant slips to individual little pots or 2 to 3 inches apart in a hotbed with the base 2 to 3 inches deep. Plants can be set into the garden 2 weeks after the last frost date.

Other starchy roots

Cassava, kudzu, malanga, taro, and yams are all starchy tropical root crops that require lots of heat and moisture and a long growing season.

NONSTARCHY ROOTS
Beets

Beets (*Beta vulgaris*) are completely edible (all parts), delicious, and rich in nutrients, making them a valuable and efficient crop for the home garden. Beets generally appreciate a cool climate and have little tolerance for hot weather. Available in ruby red, golden yellow, pink, and even striped varieties, beets are beautiful plants with dark green glossy foliage that contribute an ornamental quality to the garden.

PLANTING: Prepare a well-drained, loosened soil rich in organic material, working in compost or aged manure to increase the soil's ability to retain moisture. In early spring, as soon as the ground is workable, plant seeds $\frac{1}{2}$ inch deep and 1 inch apart in every direction. Each beet "seed" is actually a cluster of seeds; no matter how carefully you space the seed when planting, the young seedlings will need thinning as they emerge and begin to crowd each other. Harvest the thinnings, which are delicious fresh in salad or lightly steamed, gradually working toward an eventual spacing of at least 3 inches between mature beets. Beets may be successively sown every few weeks until a few months before the first expected killing frost. 50 to 65 days to maturity.

HARVESTING: For "baby" beets, carefully dig when the roots are just 1 to $1\frac{1}{2}$ inches in diameter. Mature beets should not be allowed to get larger than 3 inches in diameter or they may begin to turn woody and lose their sweet flavor. Beets that ripen in cool weather may be left in the ground, where they will hold for a long time provided they do not freeze. After harvest, remove beet greens, which may be prepared as you would chard, a close relative.

Carrots

Carrots (*Daucus carota*) are easy, quick to grow and mature, productive in a limited space, cheerily colored, delicious, and nourishing. Carrot varieties range from short, round, and stubby to long, slender, and tapering roots and come in a rainbow of colors that include orange, yellow, purple, and even white. They prefer cool, wet weather and take about 2 months to mature—a bit longer for the larger varieties, which may grow up to a foot long.

Short-rooted carrots are the best choice if you have very rocky or shallowly cultivated soil, as long-rooted carrots that encounter obstacles will stunt, twist, and fork, making them difficult to harvest and to deal with in the kitchen. Do not plant in an area that has been recently manured or has high levels of nitrogen.

PLANTING: Sow carrots in a deeply dug, finely prepared seedbed, beginning 25 days before your first frost-free date. In the South, plant in spring and fall to avoid midsummer heat. Carrot seed is fine, making it difficult to handle, and it can be slow to germinate. Sowing a mix of carrot and quick-to-sprout radish seed not only helps to mark the planting area but serves to thin and loosen the soil of the remaining carrot bed when the radishes are harvested. Keep the planting area moist throughout the growing period, and water well before thinning to prevent breakage. In areas of the country persistently plagued by carrot rust flies, sow sparsely to minimize the need for thinning. The flies, whose larvae burrow into the developing root and spoil the crop, are attracted to the carrot smell released by thinning and lay their eggs in the adjacent soil. 60 to 70 days to maturity.

HARVESTING: Carrots may be harvested early for "baby" carrots. Carefully pull or fork to avoid breakage when harvesting the tender roots. In a well-drained soil they are not ruined by slight freezing and may be mulched and left in the garden in areas with mild winters.

Parsnips

Parsnips (*Pastinaca sativa*), a pale relative of the carrot, are just about the hardest-to-grow root vegetable, but worth the trouble because of their winter-keeping ability; parsnips can handle and even thrive on being left in the garden all winter, to be dug up as needed. Their long tapered roots are covered with a smooth, light-colored skin, and their flesh cooks up soft and sweet.

PLANTING: The key to parsnip success lies in a well-prepared, rich soil; fresh seed (parsnip seed doesn't keep well for more than a year); and a cool climate. Provide a deeply dug, well-drained, sandy soil to promote long straight roots. Unlike carrots, parsnips benefit from ample quantities of manure and fertilizer. Because they are even slower to germinate than carrots, it is recommended that you similarly sow radish seeds along with the parsnip seeds to mark the planting. Wait until the soil has warmed in spring to plant, as parsnips will be even slower to emerge in a cold soil. Sow the fine seed very shallowly, ½ inch apart, and cover with ¼ inch of soil; keep the soil well watered, as parsnips will not come up through a dry soil crust. Space rows 18 to 36 inches apart depending on your available space and soil fertility. Keep plantings free of weeds throughout the growing season. 110 to 120 days to maturity.

HARVESTING: We're accustomed to rushing sweet corn from garden to cooking pot because its abundant natural sugar starts changing to starch the minute it leaves the stalk. Parsnips reverse that process: they contain lots of starch that, when the plant freezes, changes to sugar! Parsnips will get sweeter and sweeter if left in the garden over the course of a frosty winter. Begin harvesting in October by digging, not pulling, the long skinny roots from the soil. In particularly cold areas, a protective mulch will allow you to dig parsnips even when the surrounding soil is frozen.

Radishes

Radishes (*Raphanus sativus*) are the vegetable that spring-starved gardeners, anxious to get their hands in the dirt, always plant. Easy to grow and fast—you might have the first ones to eat as soon as 3 weeks after planting. The most familiar radish grown in the United States is cherry-sized, with rosy skin and peppery-hot, white flesh. Larger white radishes are generally milder than red varieties, take longer to mature, and are planted in late summer for a cool-season harvest—thus they are sometimes referred to as "winter" radishes.

PLANTING: Prepare a moisture-retentive seedbed that is not too rich. Red radishes do not require a deep soil; 6 inches is plenty, with seed sown ½ inch deep. Determine planting density by expected radish size, and thin seedlings to an eventual 2 inches apart in every direction. Because red radishes are quick to mature and do not tolerate summer heat, sow successively every 2 to 4 weeks, beginning in early spring. Plant later crops in the shade, water well, and mulch to keep cool.

Winter radishes must be planted to mature in cool weather for proper root development. Sow seed 8 weeks before the average date of your first fall frost, about 3 to 4 inches apart, and thin to accommodate spacing without crowding. If the season is dry, provide moisture to avoid tough, woody roots. 28 to 60 days to maturity depending on variety.

HARVESTING: Red radishes are one of the quickest-growing vegetables but do not hold in the garden once they are mature. Tender and crisp in their prime, within a few days they quickly turn pithy and soft. Thin and harvest the largest roots first, leaving the others to size up. Red radishes will store in the vegetable drawer of the fridge for up to a month.

Winter radishes will hold for up to 3 weeks in the garden once mature, after which time they begin to toughen. Thinnings may be used fresh like red radishes.

ASIAN RADISHES

Daikon radishes are white and substantial—2 to 4 inches across by 6 to 20 inches long—with a mild peppery taste. They are a staple in Japanese cuisine, served fresh, pickled, cooked, and carved into elaborate garnishes. Sow seed 1 inch deep in late summer for a crisp harvest throughout the fall and into winter.

Sakurajima is a large plant that needs as much room to grow as a tomato plant; its root can reach weights of 10, 20, or even 50 pounds. Extremely spicy, this variety is not eaten raw; cook as for turnips. Plant seeds 2 feet apart.

Lobak, a Korean radish, is white with pale green shading at the base, wide as a potato, and 6 to 8 inches long. Its spicy flavor is good fresh or cooked and is a part of the Korean relish called kimchi.

Chinese black radishes are long and slender like a daikon, with a black skin and white flesh; black Spanish radishes are globe-shaped. Both have a pungent flavor and may be prepared as for turnips or eaten fresh. Plant like daikon.

Rat-tail radish is grown for its long seed pods—wide at one end, dwindling to a tip at the other, thus "rat-tailed"—which develop late in the season. Harvest the bean-like pods when they are young and tender. Moderately spicy, they can be prepared like snap peas or pickled.

Wasabi is a very hot, green Japanese radish that is dried and powdered once harvested. Mix the powder with enough water to get a smooth paste and use sparingly.

Turnips and rutabagas

Turnips (*Brassica rapa*) are easy to grow and a good crop for high altitudes and chilly climates. In the South, turnips are an excellent cool-season vegetable, good for both the root and the nutritious greens.

The rutabaga (*Brassica napobrassica*), called Swede or Swedish turnip in England, is a cross between a turnip and a wild cabbage, first grown in the Middle Ages. Rutabagas thrive in cool climates and do well across the northern United States and even into the cooler parts of Canada. Grow them as you would turnips, although they get bigger and take about a month longer to mature.

PLANTING: Like any root vegetable, turnips and rutabagas like a well-tilled, fertile soil. Both dislike hot weather. Turnips may be sown 1 month before the last spring frost date for an early crop or planted in July or August for a late crop. Turnips that are grown through a hot summer will be stringy and strong tasting. In the Deep South, plant in the fall for a winter harvest. 35 to 70 days to maturity depending on variety.

In mild climates rutabagas may be planted in early spring to mature in late summer. In hot summer areas plant in June to mid-July to mature in cool fall weather; hot weather during the later part of their growth causes big tops but small, tough roots. 90 days to maturity.

Sow turnip and rutabaga seed ¼ to ½ inch deep, with 1-inch spacing in all directions. Thin turnips as they start to crowd, harvesting the thinnings for "baby" turnips, and work toward an eventual spacing of about 6 inches. Rutabagas will stunt if they are crowded; they should be thinned to 8 inches apart. Maintain soil moisture during the growing season for tender roots.

HARVESTING: Scratch the soil away from the tops of the roots to gauge size. Dig turnips beginning when they are about the size of a golf ball but no more than 3 inches in diameter. Rutabagas can get much larger without losing their quality. In mild winter areas both may be left in the ground in the fall and dug as needed. They will tolerate light frost, but repeated freezing and thawing will spoil the root.

Other Nonstarchy Roots

Jerusalem artichoke (*Helianthus tuberosus*) is a hardy perennial in the sunflower family; it has a characteristic golden blossom with a dark eye. Alternative common names are *crosne du Japon*, girasole, Japanese artichoke, sunchoke, sunroot, winter artichoke, or just plain choke—even though it's not a relative of the globe artichoke at all. Chokes are prolific growers whose tall plants can reach 8 to 10 feet. They do not suffer from insects or disease and can hold their own against any weed, but their growth must be contained or they will take over the entire garden. The crunchy white tubers of mature chokes are harvested throughout the fall and winter when the plant is dormant; any tuber left in the soil will multiply and increase to provide the following year's harvest.

Jicama (*Pachyrhizus erosus*) is a Mexican vegetable also called *sin-cama*, *sa gord*, yam bean, Mexican potato, and Mexican water chestnut. Jicama resembles a flattish turnip in both its shape and its sweet, crisp white flesh. They grow best in southern, frost-free zones, where you can harvest as needed for months, and individual tubers may get quite large. However, gardeners everywhere except the most northern tier of states can grow tubers weighing at least ½ pound.

Salsify (*Tragopogon porrifolius*) and the closely related **Scorzonera** (*Scorzonera hispanica*) are both grown for their long slender roots—white and black, respectively. Somewhat difficult to prepare in the kitchen, with a curious oyster-like flavor, these roots are not commonly grown. Cultivate as for parsnips, concentrating on cool-season growing. The flowers of mature plants are beautiful in their own right, pinkish purple (salsify) and bright yellow (scorzonera) blossoms that are a good addition to spring salads. However, do not allow the plants to set seed, as they can become invasive and weedy.

GRASSES AND GRAINS

The grass family is basic to supporting all animal life on earth. Green grass is pasture; dried grass is hay. The edible seeds of corn, wheat, rye, barley, rice, oats, and flax grasses provide grain, a rich food for both people and livestock. Millet, amaranth, quinoa, and buckwheat are nongrass plants whose highly nutritious seeds are harvested and consumed as "grain." Bamboo is a grass whose young shoots are harvested as a nutritious vegetable.

Raising your own grain may require less space than you think. Producing even a small crop of grain is not only a gardening adventure but also an instructive exercise concerning a food we typically take for granted yet is central to most people's diet.

WHEAT
Backyard wheat

Wheat (*Triticum* sp.) has been cultivated for the last 10,000 to 15,000 years, beginning in the Tigris, Euphrates, and Nile valleys. It's a good basic grain to plant. A decent crop of wheat can be produced in your own backyard if you have the right conditions and protect the tender stalks from trampling by dogs and people.

PLANTING: Wheat thrives where a cool, damp growing season is reliably followed by dry, warm days for ripening and harvest. Prepare a rich soil in full sun—conditions similar to those that would produce a good crop of corn. Broadcast seed by hand or plant in rows 4 inches apart, going back over the plot and raking to cover the seed with 1 to 2 inches of soil. Spring wheat may be sown around the time of the last killing frost and germinates best when temperatures are in the 60s. Winter wheat is planted in the fall and sprouts before going dormant with cold temperatures; growth resumes in the spring as the soil warms. Delayed plantings of either winter or spring wheat will reduce yield, as summer heat depresses grain production.

HARVESTING: Wheat is one of the slower grains to mature; it is ready to harvest when the plants have grown tall and are topped with bushy heads filled with grain seeds and the straw is just turning yellow. Winter wheat is ripe in midsummer, around 40 to 50 days from when the wheat begins to "head." Spring wheat will ripen in the fall. Harvest on a dry day, even waiting until the dew has dried. If it rains, you must wait until the grain gets completely dry again. But if you leave the wheat too long, the heads will shatter and spill the grain onto the ground. Cut, bind and tie (instructions follow) and shock to cure. Then thresh, winnow, and store. Grind as needed.

How to bind and tie a sheaf of wheat: Harvest a good-sized armload of cut straw, about 8 to 12 inches in diameter, with the grain heads all facing in the same direction. Wrap the sheaf with a handful of stalks just below the grain heads. When the band is tightly drawn around the bundle, give the two separated ends a half twist to unite them, and tuck the resulting single "rope" under the band to keep it from coming loose; this is called a *binder's knot*.

A GRAIN VOCABULARY

Chaff—the outer seed hulls of the grain that must be removed before grinding or storing. Compost the chaff or use as mulch in the garden.

Flail—a flat stick used to pound the seed heads on a hard surface free of cracks that the grain might fall into. A plastic baseball bat or a section of a rubber hose can also be used as a flail.

Shock—a teepee-shaped arrangement of individual sheaves brought together and leaned against each other toward the center, with the grain heads pointed up. Bundles of bound grain should be shocked as soon as possible after harvesting to promote further drying.

Straw—the dry stalk of the tall grass that is left after threshing the grain. Wheat straw is useful as bedding material for animals, mulch for the garden, or tilled in as a green manure.

Thresh—the process of separating the grain from the straw and the chaff. Whack the sheaves over the back of a chair, open barrel, or sawhorse, or put the grain in a sack and trample underfoot. Traditional threshing involves beating the seed heads with a flail.

Winnow—the process of separating the grain from the remnants of straw and the chaff. The easiest way to winnow is to pour the grain from a high place in a light breeze to a container below. The breeze will carry the lighter straw and chaff away. Or use a fan, which will provide any desired speed of wind at your convenience.

CORN

Corn (*Zea mays*), an annual grass with an extraordinarily high natural mutation rate, is unique among all wild grasses. Native to the Americas, it was the Native Americans who originally developed many varieties of corn through careful seed selection. The resulting flour, hominy, flint, and dent grains were the very foundation of their diet and agriculture. The Native American word for corn was *maize*, which meant "that which sustains."

Today these ancient crops, commonly referred to as *field corns* because they are left in the field to dry and stored on the cob, provide flour and ground meals as well as the most common feedstock for animals. Some colorful old-time (American) Indian flints are sold for decorative purposes and appear dried for flower arrangements or heaped in a basket as a Thanksgiving centerpiece.

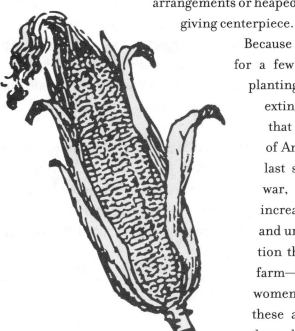

Because corn seed is only viable for a few years, you must keep planting a variety to prevent its extinction. It is remarkable that despite the vicissitudes of American history over the last several hundred years—war, western settlement, increasing industrialization and urbanization, not to mention the decline of the family farm—resourceful men and women have faithfully planted these antique breeds to keep them alive and viable.

POPCORN

Popcorn (*Zea mays* var. *praecox* or *everta*) is considered by archaeologists to be the most ancient of all corns. Slow to ripen, all popcorns mature in 95 to 120 days. In general, nonhybrid popcorn plants grow 3 to 5 feet tall and have smaller ears with small, pointed kernels; some hybrid popcorns have larger kernels. They are more drought tolerant, do not require as fertile a soil, and can handle more crowding than other varieties of corn.

Popcorn kernels have a tough outer covering (endosperm). The kernels pop when their moisture content is heated and water vapor pressure builds inside the endosperm until the whole thing explodes! There are white, black, yellow, strawberry, blue, and multicolored popcorn varieties—all turn white when popped, revealing their snowy interiors.

Sweet corn

Sweet corn (*Zea mays* var. *rugosa*) is a tasty mutation in which the kernels contain unstable sugars in a water solution as well as starch. First appearing in the 1880s, sweet corn was developed by European immigrants to the New World. Hybrid corn varieties were developed in the 1930s and became famous for their generous yield, early productivity, and ability to ripen a crop all at the same time. Although sweet corn is a good choice for commercial production, gardeners looking for an extended harvest season will need to plant several small crops of hybrid corn in succession or isolate individual plantings of early, mid-, and late-season varieties (see page 107). Home gardeners with limited growing space may want to plant an open-pollinated variety, as these tend to ripen over a period of time, giving the gardener a longer sweet corn season from a single sowing.

PLANTING: Corn requires a fertile soil and likes heat, needing at least 6 hours of full sunlight a day to thrive. Begin planting early varieties a week before your frost-free date, mid- and late-season ones 1 to 2 weeks after that date—or later. Corn will germinate better in a sandy soil that warms up quickly in the spring. Delay planting in heavy clay soils until they have warmed up to 60 to 70°F at a planting depth of 3 inches or risk losing the seed to rot. A soil thermometer will help you gauge the proper planting time. A classic heavy feeder, corn benefits from ample quantities of manure and any nitrogen-rich organic material; keep weeds down to eliminate competition for nourishment and water.

Unlike most grain, which can be sown by broadcasting, corn is planted in rows, blocks, or hills in a designated pattern and must be spaced to accommodate weeding as well as to maximize pollination; site along the north end of the garden to avoid shading other crops. Sow seed in rows 1 inch deep every 3 to 4 inches for early and midseason plantings; later plantings should be 1½ to 2 inches deep every 4 to 10 inches. For wide row plantings, space plants 10 inches apart in each direction in a bed 3 by 6 feet or 3 by 10 feet. Native Americans traditionally planted in hills or a water-collecting depression to make the best use of available water. Sow 5 or 6 seeds about 1½ inches deep in concentrations 2½ to 3 feet apart in every direction, thinning to 3 to 5 stalks per hill. Corn needs moisture to germinate and periodic irrigation or rainfall while it is actively growing, watering deeply to 4 inches.

Plants should break ground in 7 to 10 days, but note that on average, 1 out of 4 seeds won't germinate. Replant or transplant thinnings where germination has failed rather than waste the space. In very short season areas, start corn indoors 4 weeks early and move transplants into the garden 1 or 2 weeks after your last frost date, being careful to keep roots intact and undisturbed. Transplanting can be hard on corn; you may find it sulks for a week or more before it resumes growing.

From planting time until the corn is up at least a few inches, fend off hungry birds with shiny flash tape. Crisscrossed strings may further discourage them, or you can put up a scarecrow and find lots of reasons to be in the garden. Well-nourished plants and planting rotations will stave off the worst pest and disease cycles; hand-pick corn borers and earworms.

With a harvest of only 2 or 3 ears per stalk, there is no doubt that corn is a space, soil, and nitrogen hog, but many consider its garden-fresh sweetness to be worth it. Rotate where you grow corn from year to year and follow with a green manure or legume to rebuild the depleted soil's fertility.

EARLY, MID-, AND LATE-SEASON CORN VARIETIES

Early corn is 53 to 68 days to maturity and can be planted when the soil temperature is around 55 to 70°F, making it a good choice where the warm season is short. And because growing slows down in the shorter days of late summer, an early variety is also the best choice for your very latest planting. Early corn grows only 4 to 6 feet high and has smallish ears. It can be planted closer together than later corns; thin to 6 inches apart.

Midseason corn is 69 to 86 days to maturity and needs a warmer soil, 60 to 80°F. Usually the longer the corn takes to mature, the bigger the ear and the more ears you get; thin to 8 inches apart.

Late-season corn is 87 to 92 days to maturity. Growing 7 to 10 feet tall, late corn has the largest ears of any of the three; thin to 12 to 18 inches apart.

Secrets of corn pollination: Good pollination results in plump cobs filled with kernels; an ear of corn with gaps indicates kernels whose silks didn't get pollinated. Corn pollen is carried by wind from the male tassels at the top of the plant to the female silks that extend from the juvenile ear. If corn is planted in a single long row, the pollen may blow away without touching a silk; planting in short adjacent rows, or blocks, improves pollination considerably.

All corn varieties will cross with other corn varieties and affect the quality of your harvest, due to a process called "double-fertilization" in which the pollen not only determines the future heredity of that kernel but becomes half the nature of the corn kernel that will develop from that silk. For example, if a specialty "super-sweet" variety is fertilized by an unimproved variety, the resulting ears of corn will be only half as sweet as they would have been.

To avoid this, separate planting blocks by at least 250 feet or choose corn varieties that are at least 2 weeks apart in maturity dates so that flowering won't occur at the same time. Unbroken heavy rains during pollination can also interfere with or prevent normal fertilization.

HARVESTING: There is one day of absolute perfection in corn ripeness. However, you can actually start harvesting and eating several days before that day and continue several days afterward, bearing in mind that underripe corn kernels are small and flavorless, whereas overripe kernels become tough and tasteless. In general, your corn will be ready 3 weeks after the tassels begin to shed pollen; careful observation is your best clue.

- *Watch the silk.* Mature corn has dark-green husks and dried brown silk. Even if the ear still feels nice and plump, when the silk gets really dark the corn is in danger of being over-mature. If you think the silk looks dried enough, double-check by taking the next step.

- *Observe the milk.* Pull back the husk a couple of inches to see if the kernels have filled out. Puncture a kernel with your thumbnail and assess the juices or "milk." Clear milk indi-cates immature corn with undeveloped sugars; thick milk means sugars have already begun to change to starch. Some people prefer to gather ears when the milk is still thin and sweet. Some wait until the milk is white and thicker and the kernels are fuller and more mature, with a rich corn flavor.

Watch for the first ripe ears and continue to check every day or two while the harvest is on to pick the ears at their prime. The ones nearest the top of the plant generally ripen first, the lower ones later. To harvest, hold the stalk firmly with one hand as you twist and snap away the ear with the other hand. Be careful not to damage the stalk itself, because that will make it hard for the plant to finish ripening the other ears.

All fruits and vegetables taste better when garden fresh, but few are in the same class with corn in the rate of deterioration from plant to table. Once the ear is picked, its sugars immediately began to convert to starch; cool temperatures and not husking the ears until you're ready to prepare them will slow the process, but speed is of the essence. Keep the time span from field to table as short as possible for truly sweet corn. According to garden lore, you should have a pot of water already boiling when you go out to harvest corn!

THE THREE SISTERS

Native Americans traditionally interplanted corn, beans, and squash, referring to the combination as "the three sisters." Legend had it that the crops would support and benefit one another, resulting in a more plentiful harvest than if they were planted separately. You can replicate this naturally sustainable practice by spacing corn plants in close rows about a foot apart and planting several pole beans around each young stalk when it is about 6 inches tall. The corn provides a natural pole for the beans to climb, and the nitrogen fixed on the roots of the beans helps to replenish the soil after producing the corn. Shallow-rooted squash vines are planted in the area between the corn and beans as a living mulch to shade out weeds and maintain soil moisture. The fine spines on the squash vines also serve as a natural deterrent to predators after the corn and beans.

OTHER GRASSES AND GRAINS

Grain amaranth

Grain amaranth (*Amaranthus hypochondriacus* and *A. cruentus*) is grown for its seed, which closely resembles a cereal-type grain and can be treated as such.

Amaranths, a domesticated relative of pigweed, are frost-tender annuals. They are all broad-leafed plants, not grasses. The large plants, 5 to 8 feet tall, each produce a huge number of tiny seeds. Amaranth grain is high in protein and other nutrients and can be harvested and cooked like rice or popped like popcorn. The foliage is very nutritious—high in vitamin A, C, iron, calcium, and protein. Harvests vary widely depending on variety and growing conditions.

Native to the Americas, grain amaranth was nearly as important as corn and beans to pre-Columbian agriculture. Being very heat- and drought-tolerant, grain amaranth is a good crop for hot and dry areas and has been grown without irrigation in regions with as little as 7 to 8 inches of annual rainfall. Most grain amaranths are mature after 4 to 5 months, and the mature flower heads should be harvested by hand as they dry. Completely dry the "grain" before separating it from its chaff.

Bamboo

Bamboo is a primitive kind of grass native to tropical Asia; most species like warm, humid places and lower elevations. A beautiful ornamental perennial in the landscape, bamboo can also be a valuable food plant.

All species of bamboo have edible shoots, but some taste better than others. The best-tasting kinds are all varieties of *Phyllostachys*, a running bamboo that must be contained in the garden to restrict its spread. Bamboo grows amazingly fast when given fertile soil, warmth, and consistent watering. Each spring vigorous rhizomes, or underground stems, shoot out in all directions and for an indeterminate distance before sending up shoots to quickly colonize and overtake any adjacent land. Install a root-impenetrable barrier made of metal, concrete, or heavy-duty plastic 2 feet deep around your bamboo patch to control its spread, or plant in a large container.

The new shoot of the bamboo plant is eaten asparagus-style. Harvest enough every spring so your stand doesn't get too crowded, but don't take them all, as an existing grove needs new plants to stay healthy. Harvest young shoots 1 to 2 inches in diameter by cutting at ground level with pruning shears. When harvesting, be careful not to damage nearby shoots. The taller the bamboo shoots get, the less tender and edible they are.

Buckwheat

Buckwheat (*Fagopyrum esculentum*) is another exceptionally nutritious grain that is not a grass. Originally from China, it's a member of the knotweed family and more closely related to rhubarb than any of the true cereal grains. The bush-like plants grow about 3 feet high and have heart-shaped leaves. Beekeepers value a buckwheat crop for its abundant flowers that provide a good pollen source over a very long season. The resulting dark and richly flavored buckwheat honey is a prized delicacy.

Buckwheat is also a valuable green manure crop, quickly producing a thick stand of foliage capable of shading out weeds and grasses. The good-sized plants produce a generous amount of organic matter. Its tender hollow stems are easy to till into the soil, and its extensive roots are capable of breaking up and loosening sticky, dense clay.

Buckwheat grows especially well in moist, cool climates. Because heat inhibits the seed-making part of its life cycle, harvests should be timed to follow the most intense summer heat. Unlike a stand of grass grain, which ripens all at once, buckwheat continuously blossoms and will have flower buds, green grains, and ripe seed on it at any given point after midseason. To maximize your yield, harvest late enough to get as many mature seeds as possible, but before the mature plants become brittle and begin to shatter and spill their seed on the ground. Cut, bundle, shock, and thresh as described for the grass grains.

Oats

Oats (*Avena sativa*) are easy to grow and flourish in a wide range of climates and soils as long as they get ample moisture. Hull-less oats (*Avena nuda*) are the most convenient for home gardeners to thresh and grind, although the plants shatter and spill their grain more easily in the field, have a smaller yield, and are slightly more sensitive to a late spring freeze.

Mature oats are 2 to 5 feet high depending on the variety and soil fertility, with a well-filled head containing 30 to 150 grains per stalk. Cut, sheave, and shock to thoroughly dry the grain, then thresh.

Oat straw is the most nutritious of the grass grain straws for feeding animals. Oats used to be important because they were the main grain fed to workhorses. Now the usual farmload puller eats gasoline instead of oats, and everybody's worrying about Middle Eastern politics instead of the weather.

Quinoa

Quinoa (*Chenopodium quinoa*), closely related to lamb's-quarters, is a nongrass grain native to high elevations in South America, where it is a diet staple that was referred to as the "mother grain" by the Incas. Quinoa's tiny seeds are borne on dazzlingly colorful hot pink, burgundy, red, orange, yellow, white, or lime green, 4- to 6-foot plants; this is an ornamental garden standout as well as a delicious, high-protein grain.

Sow seed around spring's last frost date and when soil moisture is still high for good germination. In a moderately fertile soil quinoa is a quick grower; the young greens may be harvested and prepared like amaranth greens. By midsummer the plants will produce a sizeable seed head filled with grain; harvest when dead ripe, and dry before threshing. Moisture may cause the seed to sprout right in the head; if rain is forecast once the seed is drying, the plants should be cut, bundled, and hung to finish under cover.

LEGUMES

Peas and beans are only the most familiar members of the vast *Leguminosae* family, which are characterized by clusters of fruit that mature in pods. Legumes are highly nutritious, particularly as a protein source, and easy to cultivate, harvest, and store, making them one of the most important foods on the planet.

Legumes are great for renewing soil fertility in a crop rotation following heavy feeders. Able to draw atmospheric nitrogen and fix it in nodules along their roots, legumes make a perfect green manure; their roots should always be left in place to break down or be tilled into the soil.

Peas

Peas (*Pisum sativum*) on the vine are filled with natural sugars that, like corn, quickly begin to turn to starch once they are picked, making fresh garden peas the sweetest you'll ever taste. Choose from big peas and petit peas; dwarf bush vines and tall pole vines; spring peas, hardy "winter," or varieties that tolerate hot weather.

English or shelling peas: Common peas, referred to as English peas or shelling peas, are available in climbing or pole and self-supporting or bush varieties. Mature pods are picked and split to harvest the plump flavorful peas. Climbing pole peas take longer to mature and, depending on the variety being grown, require a 3- to 6-foot supporting structure; however, the larger vines yield more over a longer harvest period. Bush peas grow to just 2 to 3 feet; their additional wispy tendrils tangle and knit together to self-support the maturing plants, although in practice some propping will help conserve garden space.

Snow peas: Harvested before the seeds inside have begun to form, the flat pods are completely edible and widely used in Asian stir-fries or eaten fresh in salads. Snow peas are available in both bush and climbing varieties.

Snap peas: When fully mature, the juicy edible pods are filled with full-sized peas, resulting in more wonderful, unbeatable garden pea flavor without the work of shelling. Most snap pea vines require some support.

PLANTING: Impervious to cold spring weather, peas are one of the earliest crops to go into the garden. Peas like cool nights and bright, cool days; the onset of warm weather will quickly put a stop to your harvest, so it is an advantage to get plants growing at the earliest possible date for your area. Sow seed directly in the garden 1 to 1½ inches deep, 2 to 3 inches apart, in rows 3 feet apart, providing support where necessary. The large pea seeds are easy to space when planting, so thinning is unnecessary. They'll be 10 days to 2 weeks coming up, although the seeds are somewhat subject to rot if they are planted too many weeks before they germinate. Peas hate to dry out, so they require regular water throughout their growing season.

In areas where heat comes on early, plant bush peas, spacing seeds 2 to 3 inches apart in every direction in a row 18 to 24 inches wide. Planted in this way, the vines will knit together in a dense mass to shade and keep their roots cool; a single-row planting is vulnerable to drooping and failing in the heat.

For an earlier crop or to get a head start to beat the heat, pea seed may be presprouted. Spread them one pea deep in a shallow dish and add water until it comes halfway up the seed; when little sprouts show, plant immediately, before they rot. It is possible to get a fall crop with a second sowing once the peak of summer's heat has abated.

HARVESTING: Once plants have flowered, pods are quick to form and may be harvested as soon as they size up. There's no benefit to harvesting too early, as you'll cheat yourself of a full yield; however, if you wait even a few days too many, the peas will be yellow and hard and have lost their sweet taste. When picking, treat the vines gently, holding the plant with one hand as you pull off pods with the other. Well watered and carefully picked peas produce the best crop.

Beans

Beans (*Phaseolus vulgaris*) or "common" beans, often referred to as snap beans, may be prepared whole in the pod or shelled fresh or dried. Beans may be grown in any climate that has three frost-free months; in hot areas they may be planted in fall, winter, or spring.

PLANTING: Bush beans grow as a low, free-standing bush and are one of the easiest vegetables to grow, as long as you respect their temperature requirements. Early plantings may rot in very wet weather, and the plants will not tolerate even the lightest frost. Sow seed around the date of your estimated last frost, 1 inch deep and

3 to 5 inches apart in rows at least 1 foot apart. Because bush beans yield their crop intensively over a short period, planting an additional row every 7 to 10 days throughout the spring will extend the harvest period. Bush beans are a good crop for short-season climates because they are not particular about soil conditions and are ready to pick in as little as 60 days.

Pole beans are a vine with no natural built-in support for their length; instead, they opportunistically twine around whatever is at hand. Training the vines up with some means of support not only keeps them from strangling nearby plants but also is an efficient use of garden space and eases picking. Any existing trellis or fence already in the garden can be used to support bean vines; the following common devices will encourage vertical growth:

▶ *Poles:* Place 6- to 8-foot poles, 1 inch in diameter, to stand straight up with seeds planted at their base, or follow the common practice of leaning the poles together and tying them at the top to form a bean teepee.

▶ *Post and string:* Secure a sturdy post at either end of your row of beans and string a strong cord or wire horizontally between the posts at their tops and bottoms. Affix twine and string up and down between the wires to create a series of vertical runs for the bean vines to climb.

Plant the beans at the base of their support, 3 to 4 inches apart in every direction, in early summer when frost danger is completely past and the soil has begun to warm. Pole beans require a richer soil to feed the tall leafy vines; site them where they won't shade other vegetables, and give them plenty of room.

HARVESTING: Once your bush green beans start, they will bear for 4 to 5 weeks if given regular water and kept thoroughly picked. Pole beans flower and set pods from the bottom of the plant up and will continue to do so as long as the plants are well-picked until the first frost. Handle the vines gently when picking to avoid damaging the plants.

Snap beans are picked and eaten, pod and all, before their seeds have begun to mature. Most are green, but there are also purple- and yellow-podded varieties of both bush and pole beans. Wax beans are yellow with a smooth, almost translucent pod and a mild, delicate flavor. Both yellow and purple beans make for easy picking, with their bright color obvious among the leafy, green vines, and they lend an ornamental quality to the vegetable garden. Purple varieties are lovely, but be aware they turn green when cooked.

Snap beans are the most tender if they are picked before the seeds have begun to swell their pods. Some people prefer to pick them quite young and slender, in the manner of the French haricots vert. Romano beans are a European variety with large, flat, meaty pods and a distinctive flavor.

Shell beans are grown specifically for their large seeds, which are removed from the pods and either prepared fresh as green shell beans or allowed to dry and shelled for long-term storage. Nearly all shell beans are bush types; the only difference in cultivation is in their harvest methods.

SOME SHELL BEAN VARIETIES

▶ *Black beans* are Latin America's favorite bean. Also known as turtle beans, these small, glossy black beans grow on semivining bushy plants and require a warm growing season 85 to 115 days long.

▶ *Flageolet* and *horticultural beans* are bred for their large seeds, which are typically harvested at the fresh green shell stage, 60 to 75 days. They can also be dried for longer storage.

▶ *Great Northern beans* are big and white. Bushy plants produce a heavy yield in 90 days making this a good shell bean for short-season areas; they can also be harvested as green shell beans.

▶ *Kidney beans* are Mexico's most popular bean and the traditional chili bean. A white-seeded variety is called a cannellini bean. With a relatively short 95-day growing season, the kidney bean has been called the easiest dried shell bean to cultivate.

▶ *Pinto beans* are small and speckled and require a warm growing season, 85 to 105 days long. They are generally pole beans.

Other legumes

Fava beans (*Vicia faba*), also referred to as fabas (southern Europe) or broad beans (England), are easy to grow in a wet, cool climate. Favas are hardy down to 20°F, but dislike hot summers. Plant fava beans in early spring, spacing seed 4 to 5 inches apart, 1½ to 2 inches deep, in rows 12 to 36 inches apart. Bush-like plants, 3 to 5 feet tall, begin to produce plump pods 6 to 12 inches long in May and June. In the Deep South and mild coastal regions, fava beans may be planted in the fall to overwinter and begin producing much earlier in the new year. Following the initial harvest, cut plants back to 2 inches and fertilize for a secondary late summer crop. *Note: There is a very rare inherited sensitivity to fava beans and their pollen, found mostly in males of Mediterranean ancestry. This allergy, if triggered, can result in a mild to severely toxic reaction.*

Runner beans (*Phaseolus coccineus* or *P. multifloris*) are easily identified by their lush vines, colorful flowers, and "Jack in the Beanstalk" seeds, which are deep purple pink speckled in black. The runner is actually a perennial but is grown as an annual in temperate zones. They come in orange-, scarlet-, white-, and red-and-white-flowered varieties. Sow seed 2 inches deep and 6 inches apart in double rows, one on each side of a climbing support; they'll grow 10 to 12 feet high and are good for screening. They thrive in hot, humid weather and need plenty of water during their growing season. Runners can be eaten as snap beans when picked quite young and boiled or steamed. Once the pods fill out with seed they may be harvested as green shell beans or left to dry for winter storage.

Pigeon peas (*Cajanus cajun*) are an excellent garden choice if you live in the frost-free South. Woody shrubs to 8 feet tall take at least 5 months to start bearing but then will continue to produce their pretty yellow flowers and pods of small, but highly nutritious seeds for up to 5 years in a sunny location. Pigeon pea plants are dense enough that some people grow them as an edible hedge.

Southern beans or peas (*Vigna sinensis*) originated in the world's tropical regions, but can be grown in mild but warm regions, basically requiring the same climate as corn. In the United States black- and yellow-eyed peas and crowders are southern favorites that thrive in the warm days and nights of that growing region.

Soybeans (*Glycine max*) are the lowest-starch, highest-protein bean, making them a vegetarian favorite. Soybeans need heat to produce well, although some chill-tolerant kinds will produce modestly in more temperate zones. Because soybeans take a long time to mature, with a relatively small yield, homegrown crops are best enjoyed as a green shell bean, called edamame, for a high-protein snack food.

Yard-long bean (*Vigna sesquipedalis*)—also known as long bean, Chinese long bean, asparagus bean, *bodi*, *boonchi*, and *dau gauk*—is an Asian vegetable with huge yields. Climbing vines with large, pretty, lavender-white flowers produce 1½- to 2-foot-long slender beans. Closely related to black-eyed peas, yard-long beans love heat and do best in temperatures of 95 to 100°F. They're easy-to-grow, prolific producers, not usually bothered by bugs.

GOURDS

The *Curcurbit* family includes cucumbers, melons, and squashes. Along with bean and cereal crops, edible gourds were humankind's first cultivated crops. To help make garden-sense of this large and sometimes complicated botanical family, this chapter classifies plants as follows:

Cucumbers (including citron)

Melons (cantaloupe, muskmelon, and watermelon)

Squashes

    Summer squashes (zucchini and the like)

    Winter squashes (including pumpkin)

    Exotic squashes (bitter melon, calabaza, chayote,
       fuzzy melon, and spaghetti squash)

    Craft gourds

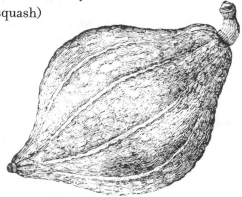

Cucumbers

Cucumbers (*Cucumis sativus*) like warm weather and lots of sunshine. Varieties include the familiar green salad cuke; thin-skinned pickling types; small, rounded yellow lemon cucumbers; and long crooked varieties from Asia. High-yielding, disease-resistant, modern cucumber hybrids produce self-fertile plants bearing only female flowers.

Citron, a cucumber relative (not to be confused with the citrus fruit that goes by the same name) looks like a small, round watermelon but has solid, uniformly green flesh and seed. Citron is generally pickled, preserved in sugar syrup, or candied and may be used when preparing fruit cakes, plum puddings, and mincemeat.

PLANTING: Cucumbers need well-tilled, fertile soil and plenty of water throughout their growing season. Put off direct sowing or setting transplants until the weather is truly warm, at least a week after your last frost date. In a very hot climate like that of the Gulf Coast, plant in early spring or late summer for a more moderate growing season. Sow seed 1 inch deep, 4 to 6 seeds to a hill, with 4 to 5 feet between hills. Garden spacing may be less if you trellis the vines to take advantage of vertical growing space. Bush varieties may be planted in hills at 3-foot intervals.

When the seedlings are 3 weeks old and well established, thin to the strongest 3 to 4 plants per hill. Do not rush this step, as young cucumbers have a fairly high attrition rate and may in fact thin themselves. Carefully weed between plants to avoid damaging

the fragile vines. Young vines are the most vulnerable to damage by pests. Control cucumber beetles by picking insects. Once they begin to grow in earnest the plants will "outrun" further damage. Most cucumbers are only 55 to 65 days to maturity, so a late start still allows time for a good crop, given a reasonably long growing season.

HARVESTING: A cucumber is 95 percent water. Once the plants begin to set fruit, water the vines deeply at least once a week, as dry conditions result in bitter fruit. Cucumbers will keep producing until the plants are killed by frost.

Melons

Melons grow best where the summer is hot, dry, and almost constantly sunny. Cloudy, rainy weather literally stops melon growth. Melons have strong taproots, which delve deep into the subsoil to find water. In a cool climate, do not irrigate, as direct watering will further cool this heat-loving plant. Nevertheless, melons require 1 to 2 inches of water a week to support their vigorous vines and produce their juicy fruit. If groundwater is such that it won't support the plants, you'll have no choice but to supplement; water only around the edge of the hill, not on the plants themselves.

PLANTING: In a northern temperate zone start plants indoors several weeks before your last frost date. Set transplants in the garden only when the weather has completely warmed and stabilized. Mulching with black plastic will help to maintain soil warmth and boost growth. In warmer growing regions melons may be direct sown 1 to 2 weeks after the last frost, when the soil has warmed.

Cantaloupe (*Cucumis melo*) describes both the smooth-skinned muskmelons and the netted-skin cantaloupes, which are grown for their sweet, fragrant pale green and orange flesh. Sow 1 inch deep, 6 feet between hills and 6 feet between rows. 65 to 90 days to maturity depending on the variety.

Watermelon (*Citrullus lanatus*) is the best fruit in the world if you're thirsty. Its crisp, juicy flesh has a tremendously high water content; people have lived with no other source of water but watermelon juice for as long as 6 weeks. Sow 1 inch deep, 8 feet between hills and 8 feet between rows. 100 days to maturity.

HARVESTING: Melons will not ripen further after picking. They may soften, but they won't get any sweeter. You haven't really tasted melon until you've had fully field-ripened fruit. Cantaloupes and muskmelons are ready to pick when the skin yellows and the fruits detach readily from the vine. The "thump test" is a reliable indication of ripeness for watermelon. Rap the fruit with your knuckles—if it sounds hollow, it's ready. White skin where the watermelon rests on the ground is also a sign of ripeness. Of course, the surest way to tell is to carve a plug from the watermelon; bright, deep pink flesh indicates sweetness and good eating.

HAND POLLINATION

All gourds typically have both male and female flowers on each plant; both sexes are necessary for fruiting to occur. Female flowers have an ovary that resembles a tiny squash or melon at the base of each blossom on a short stem; male flowers can be identified by a long, thin stem attaching the flower to the vine and a central stamen that produces pollen. Curcurbits rely on bees for pollination; without their help, fruit will be small, misshapen, or absent altogether. With today's threatened bee population or if plants are grown under cover, you may to need hand pollinate.

Often the first flush of flowers is all male, which bloom and fall from the plant without producing fruit. When plants are producing both male and female flowers, determine whether the pollen is mature—when it is, it will dust off easily on a brush or your finger. Hand pollinate in the morning, as female flowers close later in the day. Cut a mature male blossom and carefully touch its stamen to the sticky stigmas in the center of each female blossom on the plant to transfer the pollen. Some people choose to use a fine paintbrush to swirl the pollen from the stamen and swab the female stigmas.

If pollination has been successful, the young fruit will begin to form within a few days. Extreme hot or cold weather will inhibit the production of female flowers or render the pollen ineffective.

Summer squashes

Summer squashes (*Cucurbita pepo*) are grown for their young, immature fruits that are eaten whole, fresh, or cooked. Varieties include marrow, scalloped pattypan squash, yellow crookneck, and yellow straightneck and the popular zucchini. Summer squashes are notoriously prolific—especially zucchini! It blooms without fail and produces abundantly.

PLANTING: Summer squashes require warmth and a rich soil. When the soil has warmed up, well beyond the last frost, sow 2 to 3 seeds 1 inch deep in hills, with 4 feet between hills and 4 feet between rows. After germination, thin to the strongest plant on each hill. When you transplant starts take care to not disturb their roots, as the plants will suffer. Keep plantings free of weeds. 40 to 55 days to maturity.

HARVESTING: Harvest young squash at 4 to 6 inches in diameter when the skin is so tender that you can easily press your fingernail through it. Plants will continue to produce as long as they are kept picked. Large, overgrown summer squash are less flavorful, with tough skins and larger seeds.

Winter squash and pumpkins

Winter squash and pumpkins (*Curcurbita maxima*, *C. moschata*, and *C. pepo*) are allowed to thoroughly ripen on the vine, where their skin toughens to protect the sweet potato–like flesh for long storage. From a 5-pound butternut squash to a 25-pound marblehead or a 600-pound giant pumpkin, winter squashes look very different on the outside, but all are grown, harvested, and prepared in a similar way.

PLANTING: Prepare a rich bed in full sun. When the soil has warmed up, well beyond the last frost, sow 3 to 4 seeds 1 inch deep in hills 3 to 6 feet apart depending on your variety. Keep well watered and weeded, taking care to not hurt the large vines when working around them. 80 to 120 days to maturity.

HARVESTING: Winter squash and pumpkins that have cured for 10 to 14 days at 80 to 85°F after harvest will keep the best in storage. During this period the rind will harden and any surface cuts or imperfections will heal over. In many parts of the country this warm-curing period occurs naturally in the field after the vines have dried. In cooler regions, leave fruit on their vines until just after the first frost, but don't let them freeze. Cut the stems about an inch from the fruit and bring them into the warmest room in your house for curing. Once the fruit has cured, store under cool, dry conditions.

HOW TO GROW MONOGRAMMED JACK-O'-LANTERNS

When pumpkins on the vine have begun to size up but are still green and thin-skinned, incise a child's name or decoration into the skin with a sharp nail or a ballpoint pen. The shallow cuts heal into a raised scar as the skin hardens, and the result is a delight to young ones when they discover their own monogrammed pumpkins at harvest time.

Exotic squashes

Bitter melon (*Momordica charantia*), also known as *foo gwa*, balsam pear, *kareli*, and bitter cucumber, is native to Asia and India. Perennial in the tropics, it can be grown annually in zones 5 to 10, where the vine will climb to 20 feet. The fruit resembles a very bumpy, ridged light green cucumber. It does indeed taste somewhat bitter due to its natural quinine content, and it is best harvested when young, as the fruits get more bitter as they get older. *Note: Do not eat the toxic seeds of a ripe bitter melon.*

Calabaza (*Cucurbita moschata* or *Cucurbita foetidissima*) is like a large pumpkin, also called Cuban squash, *calabazilla*, and green or Indian pumpkin where it is commonly grown in Central and South America. It keeps like a winter squash and thrives in hot climates like Florida's. The large vines, to 60 feet long, produce prolifically.

Chayote (*Sechium edule*) is shaped like an avocado and is green outside but white inside. Its many names include *brionne*, *christophine*, *chocho*, mango squash, mirliton, and vegetable pear. The large vines, 30 to 100 feet a year, are perennial in frost-free climates.

Fuzzy melon (*Benincasa hispida*) is a Chinese member of the gourd family, also known as hairy melon. The many Asian varieties of this species come in various shapes. It's most comparable to our summer squash, with individual 1- to 2-pound fruits that resemble a fat green cucumber with a fuzzy, kiwi-like skin.

Spaghetti squash (*Cucurbita pepo*) is a thin-skinned fruit full of long strands of flesh instead of a solid mass like most squash. It's also, and appropriately, called vegetable spaghetti. Plant and grow like other cucurbits, harvesting when the fruits are deep yellow.

Craft gourds

Craft gourds (*Lagenaria siceraria*) or hard-shell squashes provide the makings of an easy and fun garden craft. Although inedible, craft gourds are grown for their interesting shapes and colorful patterns; growing instructions are the same as for winter squash. They are best grown as climbers over a fence or trellis so that the developing fruits can hang freely. Gardeners in the hot, dry Southwest will have an easy success both growing and curing gourds.

HOW TO GROW A LOOFAH SPONGE

Loofahs (genus *Luffa*) are a squash not eaten but used as vegetable sponges—a bathing spa favorite as well as good multipurpose scrubbers around the house. Tropical in origin, they grow best in the Deep South or may be grown in a heated greenhouse in cooler climes.

With a long growing season, loofah squash are generally started indoors several weeks before the last frost date. Soak the hard seeds for at least 12 hours and plant 2 or 3 to a 4- to 6-inch container and keep in a warm, dark place; germination can take several weeks. Once sprouted, move the seedlings into good light. When seedlings are 2 inches tall, thin to the strongest plant; at 3 inches they are ready to be transplanted outdoors, provided the weather is warm and stable. The vigorous vines are attractive, with yellow flowers.

For the best sponges, leave gourds undisturbed on the vine to mature, ripen, and dry. In shorter-season climates, harvest the gourds and dry indoors until they turn brown, feel light, and rattle with loose seeds when shaken. Slice off the big end and shake to remove the seeds. Soak the dried gourd overnight or until the skin separates from the sponge. Remove any loose pulp from the netted interior and soak in a mild bleach solution. Dry thoroughly out of direct sunlight.

THE NIGHTSHADE FAMILY

The nightshade family (*Solanaceae*) includes eggplant, peppers, and tomatoes as well as husk tomatoes, ground cherries, and tomatillos. Okra, although not a *Solanum*, grows and bears fruit in a similar manner and so is included in this chapter. All are tropical perennials that are grown as annuals in temperate zones. They take a long time to bear fruit, so northern growers must start seed indoors or rely on nurseries to provide transplants at the correct planting time. All do best when soil and air temperatures stay very warm. Nightshades grow slowly in cool weather and may be badly stunted by exposure to temperatures below 45°F. Employing a cloche, greenhouse, or other means of protective covering to retain heat is well advised before the weather warms.

Most nightshades, especially peppers and eggplant, should be hardened off; that is, slowly acclimated to outside conditions over the course of a week to 10 days before transplanting from house to garden. Each day move the seedlings in their pots to a sheltered location out of direct sun and bring them in each night. Leave them out overnight the last 2 or 3 days, provided nighttime temperatures are above 50°F.

Transplant into the garden and provide a wind screen or cloche to ensure that the young plants are not further shocked by cold.

Keep plants well watered their first few days in the garden to help their transition. Once the soil has thoroughly warmed, mulch to preserve moisture; do not apply mulch prematurely, as it will actually delay warming the soil—and postpone your subsequent harvest.

Eggplant

Eggplant (*Solanum melongena*) is a tropical perennial grown for thousands of years in China and India and since the sixteenth century in Europe. Eggplant is the most temperature-sensitive *Solanum* and botanically a "berry" (so is a pumpkin!). With a long growing season and relatively low yield per plant, eggplants may not be the most practical choice for small gardens. However, the attractive stout bushes with their lush foliage, starry purple flowers, and glossy deep purple, maroon striped, or white fruit contribute greatly to the overall beauty of the garden.

The familiar big, oval, purple variety is also called aubergine (especially outside the United States). Individual plants will yield 2 to 6 fruits, each weighing 1 to 5 pounds depending on climate and care. 80 to 100 days to maturity.

Oriental eggplants—which include Thai, Japanese, Chinese, and Indian varieties—are hardier than the aubergine, and they produce twice as many smaller fruits in a much shorter season, making them a good choice for short- and cool-season growers.

PLANTING: Eggplants thrive in well-drained, sandy, very rich soil amended with copious amounts of manure. To lessen the risk of bacterial wilt, do not plant eggplant where you have previously grown peppers or tomatoes. Start seed indoors in March or April at 75 to 90°F. Transplant into the garden 6 to 8 weeks later, well past the last frost date, and provide a plastic tunnel or cloche for additional heat and shelter from cold winds.

Space plants 18 to 30 inches apart in rows 2 to 3 feet apart. Regions with a longer and hotter growing season will produce bigger plants; provide greater spacing to accommodate. Eggplants are fairly drought tolerant. Irrigate regularly but modestly, no more than once a week, as too much water will produce watery, bland-tasting fruit. Additional feeding midseason will boost production.

HARVESTING: Aubergines typically bloom in early July but don't mature fruit until the end of August or even early September; Orientals bear earlier. Fruit that is at least as big as a large egg and has a glossy skin may be harvested or allowed to continue growing to reach full size according to the variety. Picking early also allows the plants to continue to produce. Young eggplant are more tender, with smaller seeds and no bitterness. Cut the tough stems with a sharp blade to avoid damaging the plant.

Okra

Okra (*Abelmoschus esculentus* or *Hibiscus esculentus*) is related to cotton, hibiscus, and hollyhocks. It is a beautiful plant and a favorite in the Deep South, where many gardeners plant it among their flowers rather than in the vegetable garden. It's possible to grow okra outside the South, but you must have a hot summer growing season.

Okra is a large plant, 2 to 9 feet tall, with luscious leaves that can grow to a foot wide and lovely mallow-type flowers, pure yellow or yellow with a dark eye. A particularly beautiful variety has yellow and red blooms, red stems, and red pods.

PLANTING: Okra is very cold-sensitive. It will grow anywhere as long as the soil temperature is at least 60°F, although the yield will be better in a fertile soil. In a northern garden, provide as much wind shelter as you can in an area of full sun. Plant seed directly in the garden ½ to 1 inch deep, 3 inches apart in rows 30 inches apart; dwarf varieties may be placed closer together. If you live where summers are hot but the growing season is short, sow seed indoors a month before transplanting, starting plants in a peat or paper pot that can be set directly into the garden soil to avoid disturbing the rootball. Set out plants or sow seed about the same time you would watermelon or squash, when the soil has thoroughly warmed. Thin seedlings or space transplants 12 to 20 inches apart. Whether planting indoors or out, soak seeds overnight before sowing to improve the germination rate. Keep weeds down for better production. 50 to 60 days to maturity.

HARVESTING: Severely hot, dry weather, a harsh change in temperature, or poor drainage can cause bud drop. But under the correct conditions, a few days after flowering, edible seed pods begin to form. Pick the young, green seed pods when they are 2 to 3½ inches long. Bigger pods become bitter and tough. To avoid the almost invisible spines on the plant, which cause a burning irritation, wear gloves and long sleeves, and don't pick unless the plants are completely dry.

Continue to monitor the harvest, picking regularly to keep plants producing until frost. Cut the pods rather than plucking them to prevent damaging the plants. When okra gets too tall to harvest in midsummer, southern growers cut the plants down to about 18 inches. The plants quickly grow up again and provide another crop!

Peppers

Peppers (*Capsicum* sp.) are members of a huge and varied family. Native to the Americas, peppers have been cultivated for at least 7,000 years. All peppers are tropical perennials that must be grown as annuals except in subtropical climate zones. They come in all sorts of shapes, colors, uses, and flavors ranging from mildly sweet to scorching hot. In the garden, as in the kitchen, peppers are divided by sweet and hot varieties. They have more vitamin C than citrus as well as good amounts of vitamins A, E and B1, making peppers a nutritious and flavorful addition to the table.

Hot peppers, also called chili or chile peppers, produce smaller fruit than sweet peppers on larger plants with a greater overall yield. Young fruit is green, maturing through yellow and orange stages; most end up some shade of red. The colorful plants with their peppers in various stages of ripening are often grown as ornamentals as well as for their fruit. The hotter the growing conditions, the hotter the chili; even when growing the same variety, cool northern gardens will yield a milder chili.

Hot peppers offer a range of heat from the mildly hot or semisweet to hotter hot and searing hot, all the way to the incendiary hot of the Tepin pepper, whose round, red, ¼ inch fruit, as tiny as a fingernail, is known as the hottest pepper of them all—with a Scoville rating of 600,000 units!

SCOVILLE HEAT SCALE

Food scientists and commercial food processors use the Scoville heat scale, created in 1912 by Wilbur L. Scoville, to measure the comparative spicy-hotness of foods. The scale ranges from 0 or no heat units for sweet peppers of every kind up to 600,000 units for the Tepin, the hottest pepper of them all. The chemical that makes hot peppers hot is an alkaloid called capsaicin. What the scale is actually measuring is the amount of the capsaicin present: the more capsaicin, the greater the number of heat units.

Your taste buds register sweet, sour, salty, and bitter, but when chili lovers speak of the "burn," they're being precise. The body's pain receptors perceive the literal burn caused wherever capsaicin touches the body. You "taste" hot peppers via the pain receptors in your mouth rather than the taste buds. Many chili lovers, or "hot heads," attest to experiencing euphoria similar to a "runner's high" when they eat the hottest chilies. Researchers have noted that pain receptors stimulated by capsaicin cause the brain to secrete endorphins, the same natural morphine-like chemical that is responsible for the runner's experience.

Sweet peppers come in many varieties beyond the familiar blocky bell peppers, including heart-shaped pimentos, tomato-shaped "cherry" types, and long slender tapering peppers; all have unique flavors that are delicious fresh as well as baked, stuffed, sautéed, or pickled. Green peppers, if left on the plant, will ripen to red (or yellow, dark purple, white, or brown for unusual varieties) and gain in sweetness as they mature.

PLANTING: All peppers do best with warm growing conditions. Take care to not overfertilize plants, as too much nitrogen in the soil produces tall, dark green plants with little fruit. In temperate zones, start peppers indoors about 50 to 70 days before your frost-free date, sowing seed ⅛ to ¼ inch deep. Soil temperatures of 75 to 95°F are ideal for germination; young seedlings can handle 70°F day temperatures and as low as 60°F at night. Water plants with warm water to avoid a possibly fatal cold shock. Wait to place transplants into the garden until they are at least 5 to 6 inches tall, 6 to 8 weeks old, and the last frost date is a week or two in the past. Thin seedlings or space plants 1 to 2 feet apart in rows 2 to 3 feet apart. Night temperatures below 60°F and day temperatures above 90°F will inhibit fruit set. 75 to 90 days to maturity for sweet peppers; 65 to 75 days to maturity for hot peppers.

HARVESTING: Pick peppers to keep plants producing at full capacity; hot peppers gain in heat with maturity. When frost is imminent, pull up the whole plant, bring indoors, and hang upside down to continue to ripen the fruit. *Note: Wear gloves when harvesting or processing hot peppers. Whenever working with cut chilies, keep your hands away from your face, especially your eyes. Keep all chilies—whole, cut, or ground—out of reach of small children!*

Tomatoes

Tomatoes (*Lycopersicon lycopersicum* aka *L. esculentum*) are fruit, botanically speaking. In 1893 the U.S. Supreme Court applied its solemn expertise to the problem of tomato classification and decided that henceforth the tomato would legally be a vegetable rather than a fruit. In the end, tomatoes are a versatile fruit/vegetable with many delicious applications and are the most popular garden vegetable grown in the United States.

A tropical native of South America, tomatoes perform best with a long, hot growing season, but through rigorous selection and hybridizing seed companies have developed varieties for nearly every climate, zone, and garden condition.

Tomatoes come in red, orange, pink, green, or white, with fuzzy or smooth skin. They range from super-sized beefsteak tomatoes, which can weigh in at $1\frac{1}{2}$ to 2 pounds, to cherry or tiny currant-sized fruit, some of which are as small as a marble or a pea. They can be sweet or sour, round or oval, open-pollinated heirloom varieties whose garden history goes back 100 years or more or brand-new, heavy-yielding hybrids. Early varieties set fruit well even in cool weather and mature quickly; mid- and late-season tomatoes bear the largest individual fruits but take longer to mature.

PLANTING: Prepare a bed in full sun with fertile soil. Tomatoes need a soil temperature of 60 to 85°F for best germination. If you live in the southern part of Florida or Texas, you can plant directly into the garden, sowing seed $\frac{1}{2}$ inch deep; plant generously and thin to the strongest plants. In temperate zones, start tomatoes indoors 6 to 8 weeks before your frost-free date. Sow seed $\frac{1}{4}$ inch deep and cover pots or seed flats with newspaper, plastic, or glass to maintain high humidity and darkness. Maintain a temperature of at least 70°F and keep the soil moist with a fine spray. When seedlings emerge, remove the cover and provide lots of light.

When the seedlings are 3 to 4 inches tall, repot into a deeper container, setting plants down in the soil right up to the leaves. Depending on the weather, plants may need to be repotted once more before being thoroughly hardened off and set into the garden.

With some form of protective covering to retain heat, tomatoes may be transplanted into the garden 3 weeks before the last frost date. Water seedlings well and plant in trenches to make the most of the warmth in shallow soils. Pinch off the lowest leaves and set the plants horizontally in shallow furrows 4 to 6 inches deep, with only the tops of the plants protruding from the soil. These buried stems will develop roots along their entire length; a bigger rootball means a larger and sturdier plant with a greater yield. Set plants 2 to 6 feet apart depending on your chosen training method; do not mulch until the soil is thoroughly warmed, unless you are using black plastic.

If tomato disease is a problem in your growing region, select varieties that are resistant to verticillium wilt, fusarium wilt, or nematodes, indicated by V, F, and N codes on seed packets. To avoid disease, rotate your tomato crop in the garden each year and wait 3 years before planting tomatoes in the same place or in a place where peppers, potatoes, or eggplants have grown.

Tomatoes are fairly pest-free in the garden, save for those parts of the country that must deal with the tomato hornworm—a very fat, 1½- to 3-inch-long, hairless green grub with one horn sticking out of its tail. A truly remarkable sight and a pest that can wreak great damage on your tomato plants; control by picking early in the day when most of the grubs are concentrated deep within the plants. You'll have to look closely as they may be utterly camouflaged by their bright green color, which blends with the surrounding tomato foliage.

Tomatoes are self-fertile and insect-pollinated. If the crop is grown under cover, gently rustle the plants with your hand to encourage their "perfect" flowers, which contain both male and female parts, to self-pollinate and increase yield.

TRAINING TOMATOES

Tomatoes are categorized by their growth habit. Determinate varieties are stout bushy plants, 18 to 30 inches tall, that flower and bear fruit all at once. Indeterminate plants are large vines to 6 feet that continue to grow, flower, and set fruit until frost. These large vines may be allowed to sprawl over the ground or more typically are caged, staked, or trellised to conserve garden space and expose the ripening crop to the sun.

Staking plants entails training 2 to 3 strong "leaders" or stems up a single stake placed in the ground near the tomato at planting time or against the support of a trellis or fence. Gently tie the vines to their support as they extend, taking care not to damage the stem. Prune to remove excess foliage and suckers that emerge from leaf axils; this helps expose ripening fruit to the sun. Individually staked plants do not produce as heavily as caged or free-rein plants; however, they may be placed at closer intervals in the garden for a good yield per square foot overall.

Caged plants are encircled with a cylinder of wire fencing (or a commercial tomato cage) and plants are trained up through the cage with their branches supported by side rungs. Cages should be about 2 feet in diameter and 4 feet in height; stake cages on either side to secure them, as mature plants are heavy and you don't want the cages to topple.

HARVESTING: Vine-ripened tomatoes are such a treat—true edible perfection! Fruit will color up and begin ripening in late July or August depending on the variety and your growing conditions. Pick them as soon as they are ready, and the plants will continue to produce until frost. Plants may be shielded from light frost if draped with protective plastic sheets. When the weather turns for good and the season is over, dig up the plants, bring them indoors, and hang them upside down to continue to ripen the fruit.

GREEN TOMATOES

Tart, crunchy green tomatoes star in their own tasty recipes and are a southern tradition. Light, selective harvesting of immature green tomatoes will grant you two crops from a single planting, but fall frosts usually leave at least some immature tomatoes in all gardens. To test, slice a green tomato with a sharp knife and try to cut one of its seeds in two. Tomatoes that have matured have seeds suspended in a jelly-like juice that will shift away from the knife so the seeds don't get cut. A tomato that hasn't matured its seed will not ripen off the vine and is best prepared "green."

Other nightshade family vegetables

Ground cherry (*Physalis peruviana*), also called strawberry tomato or husk tomato, is not a true tomato. This low, bushy plant bears round yellow fruit about the size of a small cherry inside a thin, paper-like husk. Native to the Central and South American tropics, there are several wild and domestic species, but the most flavorful is generally referred to as the giant ground cherry or cape gooseberry. Ground cherries have a delicious sweet fruity flavor often likened to pineapple. They will grow in poor soil and need little care; follow procedures for planting and growing tomatoes. Harvest ground cherries when they have turned yellow and become a little soft. Expect about 75 days to maturity and about 2 pounds of fruit from each plant.

Tomatillo (*Physalis ixocarpa*), also called Mexican husk tomato, is closely related to the ground cherry and available in green and purple varieties. Green types bear larger fruit that is 2 to 2½ inches across, but purple varieties, although only 1 to 1½ inches across, taste and store better. Their sweet-tart flavor is a key ingredient in Mexican food and savory salsas. Tomatillos grow encased in a papery outer husk that splits when the fruit is ripe; pick when the fruit are the size of walnuts. With only 68 days to maturity, tomatillos are ready more quickly than tomatoes, don't mind cooler weather, and are prolific producers.

HERBS

Aromatic and flavorful herbs mark the changing seasons, from sweet oniony chives of early spring through lavender, thyme, sage, and rosemary, pungent Mediterranean natives of summer, to the heady perfume of a late summer basil harvest. Herbs add a rich sensual dimension to even the most basic diet. A great many herbs may be grown in a small garden all their own, a garden tradition since the Middle Ages. They may be used to outline ornamental borders or planted in and amongst vegetables, where their inherent pest-resistant properties are put to good use, or simply tucked into a window box or container on the back porch. Wherever you grow them, keep herbs handily near the kitchen where you can easily snip a tip for a fresh salad, steep a cup of tea, or concoct a perfumed pesto and allow them to work their delicious magic on everyday meals.

Although some herbs may be planted from seed, many are best purchased as starts from your local nursery or a shared division from a generous neighbor, because seed strains of many herbs may vary in the intensity of their flavor from plant to plant. Most nursery varieties have already been selected for their superior flavor; however, don't hesitate to pinch, sniff, and sample when choosing plants to select those with the strongest aroma and flavor.

Most herbs are not fussy about the soil they are grown in, asking only for good drainage, sun, and good air circulation. Resist the urge to fertilize your backyard herbs; this may get you larger plants, but often at the expense of bold flavor, as growth dilutes the essential oils that lend them their character. When harvesting, gather the herbs on a dry day, early in the morning once the dew has dried. In most cases, the young leaves of plants before they flower are at their peak flavor.

Their beauty is not obvious or showy, but there is a simple prettiness to an herb patch—with its many shades of green and its small flowers mostly in shades of pink or lavender, with the occasional blue thrown in—that is a satisfaction to the eye and the palate. Many gardeners will tell you no kitchen garden is complete without the addition of fresh herbs.

Angelica

Angelica (*Angelica archangelica*): This hardy biennial is best sown from seed, as the sturdy taproot does not transplant well unless very young. Plants will form a small leaf rosette in their first year before shooting up 6 to 8 feet tall the following year. The stout, hollow, self-supporting stems are clothed with lush 2- to 3-foot-long toothed leaves, and mature plants produce white, lacy dill-like flowers before setting seed and dying. Provide a good soil and constant moisture in full to partial sun.

> USES: The young leaves in spring have a delicate, sweet celery-like flavor that may be added to salads and stock or roasted with other aromatics. The candied stems are a traditional herbal sweet.

Balm, lemon

Also called sweet balm, lemon balm (*Melissa officinalis*) is a hardy perennial herb, growing 2 to 3 feet tall with tiny white flowers and lemony-mint flavored leaves. A golden-leafed form is especially attractive. A close relative to mint, lemon balm spreads by runners and can also seed around aggressively. Keep plants cut back and harvest the young growth often to prevent flowering. Plant in damp, fertile soil in partial shade.

USES: The leaves make a lovely herbal tea that is refreshing iced and is said to relieve headaches.

Basil

A favorite summertime herb with a spicy perfume and clove-like flavor, this annual is easy to grow from seed or starts. Basil (*Ocimum basilicum*) requires a rich fertile soil and warmth; it will not tolerate cold weather, collapsing into a blackened mush at the first touch of frost. It's a good herb for container gardening. With green and purple leaf varieties, large and small habits, and nuanced flavors including cinnamon, lemon, and spicy Thai, there is a basil for every taste.

USES: Traditional sweet basil is the foundation for Italian pesto and marries well with tomato dishes. Harvest tender stems and leaves regularly to prevent flowers from forming; the plant will branch and continue to produce throughout the season.

Bay

This evergreen tree can get quite large, is not fussy about soil, and can take full sun to mostly shade. Hardy to about 10°F, sweet bay (*Laurus nobilis*), as it is commonly called—not to be confused with California bay (*Umbellaria californica*)—is an excellent container plant and may be kept formally clipped to curtail its size. Establish nursery plants in the garden, providing well-drained soil and shelter from severe winter winds and extreme cold temperatures.

> USES: Use fresh or harvest leaves and dry for storage. Remove leaves from the finished dish, as they are tough and difficult to digest. A traditional herb for soup, hearty stews, and meat dishes, bay also lends a sweet herbal flavor to cream-based desserts.

Bee balm

The shaggy blossoms of this North American hardy perennial herb are a favorite of hummingbirds and strongly attractive to bees. Purchased plants may be installed in the garden in the spring or fall, preferring a fertile, moist soil in partial shade. Bee balm (*Monarda didyma*) grows 3 to 4 feet tall, has a tendency to spread by runners, and should be divided every 3 years.

> USES: The aromatic leaves are the most strongly scented right before the plant flowers. Their lemony-mint flavor makes a delicious tea and is good minced in fruit salad. A beautiful addition to any garden, bee balm offers good support for pollinators.

Borage

This easy-to-grow ornamental and edible annual herb has bristly, cucumber-flavored leaves and numerous lovely, intensely blue flowers that attract bees. Borage (*Borago officinalis*) has a lax, informal habit, growing to 24 to 30 inches, and has a tendency to casually self-sow around. Sow seed directly in not-too-fertile soil in partial shade.

> USES: Harvest the younger leaves before the bristles become too pronounced, although a vinegar-based dressing or the heat of cooking will dissolve the fine hairs. The beautiful starry blue flowers make a charming and edible garnish for salads and cool drinks.

Burnet, salad

An attractive perennial herb most often included with ornamental plantings, salad burnet's (*Poterium sanguisorba* or *Sanguisorba minor*) low mound of cucumber-flavored, toothed foliage flourishes from early spring long into the fall. Wiry stems are topped by tiny button flowers of a deep wine color. Plants may be grown from seed or nursery starts; provide a rich, well-drained soil that receives at least 6 hours of sun a day.

> USES: The young tender leaves are used fresh in salads and cream-based soups or as a flavoring for a mild vinegar. Keep the plants well picked, as the leaves become bitter with age.

Catnip

This perennial, with its somewhat fuzzy gray-green leaves and spires of lavender or white flowers, is notoriously favored by felines. Being in the mint family, the tough catnip (*Nepeta cataria*) plant will survive the predation and nibbling of ecstatic cats, quickly recovering from even the most dramatic mowing. Plants may be grown from seed or purchased as transplants. Provide full sun and regular moisture throughout the growing season.

> USES: In addition to providing countless hours of enjoyment for our pet companions, catnip makes a soothing and calming tea for humans.

Chamomile, German

This airy, upright annual has fine-needled foliage and small white daisy-like flowers. Sow seed directly in the garden in and amongst vegetables and other herbs. If some of the flowers are allowed to set seed, German chamomile (*Matricaria recutita*) will self-sow for repeat crops.

Chamomile, Roman

A low, mat-forming perennial groundcover, Roman chamomile (*Chamaemelum nobilis*, or *Anthemis nobile*) has fragrant ferny foliage and small white daisy-like flowers in summer. Evergreen in most climates, Roman chamomile has been used as lawn substitute, as it takes well to light foot traffic and needs little mowing. Purchase plants and establish in a fertile soil in full sun to partial shade.

> USES: For all that the two plants are unrelated, both German and Roman chamomile flowers make a relaxing "sleepy-time" tea with a sweet apple fragrance.

Chervil

This hardy annual grows 1½ to 2 feet tall. Delicate, feathery foliage has a mild tarragon flavor. Sow seed directly or purchase starts; chervil (*Anthriscus cerefolium*) is easy to grow in poor soil as long as plants receive regular water. Protect from hot afternoon sun.

USES: Harvest the young leaves for use in salads, soups, sauces, and wherever you would use parsley or tarragon.

Chives

For chives (*Allium schoenoprasum*), see the Allium section.

Cilantro

Also referred to as coriander, Chinese parsley, and Mexican parsley, cilantro (*Coriandrum sativum*) is a hardy annual easily grown from seed; succession sow every few weeks for a constant supply of fresh leaves. Allow a few plants to flower to harvest their subsequent crop of seed. Keep flower stalks picked off of remaining plants to keep them producing new foliage.

USES: Leaves are used fresh and are a staple in Mexican and Indian cuisines. Dried seeds may be added to breads, desserts, and spice mixtures. Cilantro leaves have a strong taste that diners tend to either love or hate, so it's a kindness to check with your guests before including it in your planned menu.

Comfrey

This deeply rooted, perennial herb has recently become controversial. At one time comfrey (*Symphytum officinale*) was a traditional cure for just about anything from broken bones to skin conditions, but modern chemistry has identified it as containing pyrrolizidine, a poisonous substance, and experts recommend that comfrey should not be ingested in any way. However, the plants, which are almost impossible to eradicate once established, are rich in nutrients and make a good organic mulch or fertilizer tea in the garden.

Dill

This common garden herb is an annual with feathery leaves, little yellow flowers, and a flavor strongly associated with pickles. Directly sow in the garden and maintain soil moisture throughout the season; dill (*Anethum graveolens*) may flower prematurely if allowed to dry out.

USES: Cut the fine foliage, called dill weed, to include in salads, sauces, and vegetable, egg or fish preparations. Flower heads may be picked at any time before the seeds have formed and are traditionally included when canning dill pickles; the plants will continue to put out more flowers. To harvest the stronger-tasting dill seed, cut the plants before the seed heads turn dark brown and hang to dry in a dark area with good air circulation. Provide a sheet or papers beneath the hanging bunch to catch any seed that falls.

Fennel

A striking, perennial herb that grows 3
to 5 feet tall, fennel (*Foeniculum vulgare*)
is grown for its fine dill-like foliage, deep
yellow pollen, and aromatic seeds, all of
which have an earthy licorice-like flavor.
(It should not be confused with Florence fennel, discussed in the Stems section.) Plant in full sun
where it will not crowd other crops and can remain undisturbed for years

> USES: The foliage is best harvested when it is young and
> tender for use in salads, sauces, and fish preparations.
> Pollen is collected from the fresh umbel blossoms for
> use in any dish that requires a delicate touch; the ripe
> green seeds have a stronger flavor and may be used fresh
> or dried.

Lavender

This small, woody subshrub is a perennial favorite in herb gardens
for its sweetly aromatic foliage and beautiful purple-blue flowers that
bloom throughout the summer. Lavender (*Lavandula* sp.) thrives best
in hot sun and a light, dry soil; winter losses are more likely attributable
to wet weather than to cold temperatures. Depending on the variety,
plants grow 1 to 3 feet tall and as wide. Shear the plants when harvesting
the flower stems to promote well-branched growth.

> USES: The blossoms are used fresh or dried in jelly, in fragrant
> potpourri, and as a moth repellant; they are a component of the
> traditional French herb mix *herbes de Provence*, along with rose-
> mary, marjoram, basil, bay, and thyme.

Lemon verbena

This attractive woody shrub bears sprays of tiny pink flowers and long, pointed light green leaves that smell and taste strongly of fresh lemon. Provide full sun and a fertile soil; lemon verbena (*Aloysia triphylla*) is drought tolerant once established but not likely to be winter-hardy in climates that get hard freezes.

USES: The leaves have the strongest flavor in late summer but can be picked at any time for use in fruit salads, iced and hot teas, and desserts or dried for storage over the winter.

Lovage

Similar in culture, size, and habit to angelica, lovage (*Levisticum officinale*) can be grown similarly, starting from seed in late fall or early spring.

USES: The leaves and seeds may be used wherever a strong celery flavor is desired. Lovage provides a dramatic focal point in the garden and offers good support to bees and other beneficial insects.

Marigold, pot

A hardy annual flower, pot marigold's (*Calendula officinalis*) Latin name refers to its propensity to bloom in almost every month of the calendar year. Bright, multipetaled blossoms in the warm colors of the sun are produced on plain green plants that grow to about 18 inches.

USES: The colorful petals may be included in mixed herb salads or brewed to create a strong tea. An ointment or balm infused with calendula is very soothing and used to treat inflammation and wounds.

Marjoram, sweet and Greek oregano

Native to the Mediterranean, both sweet marjoram (*Origanum majorana*) and Greek oregano (*Origanum heracleoticum* or *Origanum vulgare* ssp. *hirtum*) prefer a well-drained soil in full sun. (Other plants labeled *Origanum* are either ornamental varieties or weak in flavor; Italian oregano is a cross between sweet marjoram and Greek oregano, with the flavor of the former and the tougher constitution of the latter.) Neither species is either completely hardy or very long lived, so it is best to replace plants with fresh starts every couple of years, if not every year, depending on your climate. Plants are 1 to 2 feet high and clothed with tiny, aromatic gray-green leaves with small lavender or white flowers in summer.

> USES: Harvest leaves for use in classic Italian preparations and savory soups and stews as well as vegetable, egg, and cheese dishes. Marjoram is unusual in that its flavor is actually improved by drying.

Mint

These very hardy perennials can be overly aggressive in the garden due to their spreading roots and colonizing ways. All mints (*Mentha* sp.) need steady watering throughout the season and will tolerate partial shade. Purchase plants or get a start from a mint-growing neighbor— they'll have plenty to share! The following is a list of various mints, each with their own character: apple mint, ginger mint (green and gold foliage), peppermint, orange mint, pineapple mint (green and white foliage), and the most common culinary mint, spearmint.

> USES: Cut the leaves and tender stems at any point during the plant's growth for use in salads, sauces, teas, and sweets.

Parsley, curly and Italian

This popular deep green, biennial herb does well just about anywhere. Seeds can be notoriously slow to germinate, so most gardeners start with nursery plants. Transplant carefully so as not to damage the long, sensitive taproot. Curly parsley (*Petroselinum crispum*) grows 8 to 10 inches tall and keeps fresh longer once cut; Italian (*Petroselinum crispum* var. *neapolitanum*), or flat-leaf parsley, is taller, stronger in flavor, and hardier over the winter, standing through all but the most severe freezes. Parsley will flower in its second year, turn bitter, and go to seed; discard plants and start over.

USES: Once relegated to use strictly as a garnish, today parsley is appreciated for its fresh, grassy "green" flavor and high nutrient value. It is used liberally in salads, vegetable dishes, tonic juices, and many other preparations.

Rosemary

This decorative, somewhat tender woody shrub has leaves like soft green needles. In moderate climates, upright forms may be planted as informal hedges; trailing forms will spill down rockeries, over a wall, or from a hanging basket. Delicate blue flowers bloom on branch tips in early spring, with some repeat bloom in the fall. Plant nursery starts in light, well-drained soil in full sun. Rosemary (*Rosmarinus officinalis*) is tolerant of heat but does not do well under humid conditions.

USES: Harvest the needles at any time throughout the year to use fresh. Rosemary has a strong, distinctive flavor and should be added to preparations in small amounts, tasting after each addition, to avoid overpowering the finished dish. Stems may be dried for storage, and the wood is sweetly fragrant when added to an open fire or barbecue.

Sage

A savory, semihardy woody perennial that grows to 2 feet high and as wide, sage (*Salvia officinalis*) is evergreen in frost-free climates. Spikes of lavender-blue flowers appear in summer. Variegated, purple, and golden-leaved varieties lend an ornamental quality to the garden.

> USES: The broad, oval leaves have a camphorous flavor that enhances poultry, cheese, and egg dishes. Leaves may be used fresh or harvested and dried.

Sage, pineapple

This tender perennial has a character very different from that of its broad-leaved cousin. Transplant nursery starts into the garden after the last frost and provide a well-drained soil in full sun. Plants can grow 4 to 6 feet in a single season. Pineapple sage (*Salvia elegans*) is often the last herb of the season to bloom, producing its bright red-orange blossoms in early fall. It's a favorite of hummingbirds, so many gardeners plant pineapple sage just to attract these antic birds to their garden. Both the flowers and the tender, somewhat fuzzy leaves are edible, with a sweet flavor likened to pineapple. A close relative, fruit sage (*Salvia dorisiana*) has distinctive large lime-green leaves and pinky red flowers; it may be used in the same way.

> USES: The leaves and flowers of both these sages are good in fruit salads, juice, and herb jellies.

Savory, summer

An 18-inch-tall annual, summer savory (*Satureja hortensis*) is easily grown from seed. Prepare a light soil in full sun and succession sow throughout the spring for a constant harvest of tender leaves.

USES: See the entry for Savory, winter.

Savory, winter

This hardy perennial survives down to 10°F if mulched in a sheltered position. Smaller in stature than summer savory, winter savory (*Satureja montana*) displays lavender flowers throughout the summer.

Both plants attract bees, prefer full sun, do well in poor, stony soil, and prefer to dry out between waterings. The flavor is strongest when the plants are in flower. Summer savory leaves can be harvested in mid-summer or can be pulled out by the roots in the fall for drying. Harvest the tips of winter savory 2 or 3 times a summer to use fresh or dry.

USES: The leaves of both types of savory have a peppery quality that goes well in salads, soups, and sauces. Dried leaves are good in poultry stuffing and with meats, fish, cheese, eggs, and green beans.

Tarragon, French

This somewhat tender, short-lived perennial must be mulched well where winters are severe. Slender stems 2 to 3 feet long are clothed with narrow leaves with a delicate anise flavor. True French tarragon (*Artemisia dracunculus*) does not flower or set seed in temperate climates, so plants must be purchased as nursery starts. (Russian tarragon, a much taller and coarser plant that readily flowers and sets seed, is inferior in flavor and not recommended.) Provide a well-drained, fertile sandy soil in full sun to partial shade.

> USES: Widely used in French cuisine, tarragon is a good match with eggs, cheese, seafood, and many sauces.

Thyme, common and lemon

This popular, semi-hardy, low-growing Mediterranean perennial comes in a host of varieties. These two are the ones best suited for kitchen use. Common thyme (*Thymus vulgaris*) grows 6 to 12 inches tall with gray leaves and lavender blooms. It is evergreen in areas with mild winters and makes a good edging plant in herb gardens. Lemon thyme (*Thymus citriodorus*) grows 4 to 12 inches high with green or green-and-yellow leaves and lavender blooms and has a subtle lemon flavor that dissipates quickly when heated. Lemon thyme is not quite as hardy as common thyme. Purchase nursery starts and plant in full sun to partial shade. Poor soil and infrequent watering actually improve thyme's flavor.

> USES: Snip the tips of the leafy branches often, both for use in the kitchen and to keep the plants well branched and bushy. Thyme dries easily and suffers no loss of taste in the process. Both common and lemon thyme have innumerable kitchen applications, matching up well with a wide variety of foods; the only caveat is to add a pinch at a time and taste as you go, because thyme is a strong flavor capable of overpowering a finished dish.

Watercress

A peppery, sharp-flavored herb that adds zest and tang to salads. Low, leafy clumps require shade and a damp to wet soil, growing best alongside a stream bank with a constant flow of cool, clean water. Watercress (*Nasturtium officinale*) may be grown in containers that receive daily watering, but it will not be as succulent.

> USES: Harvest individual leaves in a cut-and-come-again manner or cut the entire plant at its crown. Watercress is at its best and mildest in cool weather before plants flower. Add to salads, sandwiches, and mayonnaise-based sauces.

CARLA'S LEGACY

Carla Emery grew up on a sheep ranch in Montana and was educated at Columbia University. In the early 1970s she settled on a farm in northern Idaho, where she wrote the first edition of *The Encyclopedia of Country Living*. Originally entitled *Carla Emery's Old Fashioned Recipe Book* and produced on a mimeograph machine in her living room, the book launched its author to the forefront of the back-to-the-land movement.

Growing Your Own Vegetables is the first in a series of single-subject guides drawn from material that appears in *The Encyclopedia of Country Living*, now in its tenth edition. I'm pleased, proud, and delighted to have been asked to author these works for many reasons—not the least of which is my growing fascination with writing about gardening and food, but also because—as my editor put it—I "understand the ethos" of what Carla set out to accomplish when she began so many years ago.

In Seattle during the 1960s and 70s, while Carla was girding herself for society's collapse, I was riding my Sting-Ray bike, hula-hooping, and bopping to AM radio, blissfully oblivious about the world's superpowers flexing their nuclear muscles. After college, in a somewhat belated "flower child" period marked by a fierce streak of independence,

I purchased one of Carla's earliest editions. I was determined to bake our bread and grow our food. However, life in the city is forgiving—if something went awry or I got tired, we simply went out to eat! This was hardly the stuff of self-sufficiency, but still reflective of my desire to be a part of the process and an early awareness of a food web growing increasingly industrial and removed from daily life.

Thankfully, at present, the pendulum is swinging the other way. Increasingly our eyes are open to where our food comes from and how it is produced. More and more, clean, healthy food; safe, sustainable growing practices; and fair living conditions are attracting mainstream concern.

Carla Emery remained a tireless advocate of self-sufficiency and environmental stewardship until her death in 2005. Today's "green living" movement owes a tremendous debt of gratitude to Carla and others like her, who never gave up their pursuit of a good and healthy existence. These contemporary pioneers resuscitated and breathed new life into the skills and traditions of our grandparents and their parents. We may not have more than a tiny patch in the backyard or a few containers on a shyly proportioned patio, but there is still plenty we can grow . . . and plenty more we can learn in the process.

Lorene Edwards Forkner—freelance writer, garden designer, and food enthusiast—revels in the seasonal pleasures and broad scope of gardening in the Pacific Northwest. She is currently at work on additional titles drawn from material found in The Encyclopedia of Country Living. *Follow her work by visiting her Web site, PlantedatHome.com.*

ACKNOWLEDGMENTS

Many thanks are due to Sasquatch Books and the company's enduring commitment to providing gardeners—and people who love to eat—with books that inform, inspire, and educate those wishing to dig in the dirt. The important work of Carla Emery and the contents of her *Encyclopedia of Country Living* are sustained by their efforts. Thank you to Gary Luke, my editor at Sasquatch, for inviting me on the adventure.

Thank you to Chris Curtis of the Neighborhood Farmers Market Alliance who, along with her industrious staff, has done so much to bring fresh food to Seattle neighborhoods, including to my own, wonderful West Seattle farmers market.

Thank you to Matt and Leda Langely of Langely Fine Gardens on Vashon Island for their ardent devotion to providing an amazingly varied (and delicious) list of organic vegetable starts for home growers. From 'Green Zebra' tomatoes to tiny alpine strawberries and 'Cavolo Nero' kale, my plot—and my plate—is richer for their efforts and their expertise.

A passion for growing our own food is a constant that unites generations and bridges political and economic boundaries. From ornery

Bill—my neighborhood farmer, his wheelbarrow laden with produce—to the twinkling eyes of my young son and his bean in a Dixie cup, the magic of cultivating fresh fruits and vegetables is lost on no one. It is exciting to watch the public's return to the vegetable garden. Actively participating in the creation of an organic, sustainable, lively, and fresh food system is good for our health as well as the well-being of our planet and our communities.

—LEF

APPENDIX:
HOW TO MAXIMIZE YOUR GARDEN'S YIELD

Succession planting keeps the garden in constant production. Cool-season crops like peas, spinach, or early lettuce may be planted as soon as the soil is workable in the spring and are harvested before the onset of summer heat. These are followed up by a sowing of warm-season beans or corn, or planted with transplants of tomatoes, peppers, and squash. Either method allows a second crop to be produced in the same space within a single growing season. Areas with mild winters may even follow a warm-season planting with another cool-season crop to produce throughout fall or over winter for an especially early spring harvest the following year.

Cool-season plants thrive in the moist, chilly days of spring and fall to produce leaves, stems, and roots that are harvested while still young and tender. In general, warm-season crops require long, hot, sunny days to flower, fruit, and ripen. Coastal and northern gardens can produce cool-season crops throughout the entire growing season, but may require heat-saving devices and weather protection to produce warm-season crops. Hot summer regions will yield warm-season crops with little additional protection, but may require partial shade or planting in the cooler seasons of spring or fall to produce cool-season crops. Those plants that tolerate both cool and warm weather are resilient and oftentimes very productive crops that will yield over a very long season.

COOL SEASON PLANTS

Asparagus*	Florence fennel	Peas
Broccoli	Globe onions	Potato
Broccoli raab	Kohlrabi	Radish
Brussels sprouts	Leek	Rhubarb*
Cabbage	Lettuce	Scallions
Chinese cabbage	Mizuna, mustard & arugula	Sea kale*
Chives/garlic chives*		Spinach
Corn salad	Parsnip	Turnips & rutabagas

WARM SEASON PLANTS

Amaranth	Cucumber	Quinoa
Artichoke & cardoon*	Eggplant	Runner beans
Bamboo*	Fuzzy melon	Southern peas
Beans	Ground cherry	Soybeans
Bitter melon	Jerusalem artichoke*	Summer squash
Buckwheat	Jicama	Sweet potato
Calabasa	Melon	Tomatillo
Cauliflower	Okra	Tomato
Chayote	Peppers/sweet & hot	Winter squash & pumpkins
Corn	Pigeon peas*	
Craft gourds	Purslane	Yard long beans

*perennial plants with permanent garden placement

COOL AND WARM SEASON PLANTS

Beets	Collards	Orach
Bunching onion*	Fava beans	Swiss chard
Carrots	Garlic & shallots	Wheat
Celeriac	Kale	
Celery	Oats	

Another way to make a small garden "work bigger" is to take advantage of the space between slower-to-mature vegetables by planting a crop that is quick to mature. For instance, plant lettuce, spinach, arugula, radishes, baby carrots, and beets between rows of the slower-growing winter squash or melons. These "catch crops" are quick to mature before the neighboring vines sprawl to fill in their growing space. Similarly, fall crops of broccoli, kale, and cabbage are easier to get started in the cooler shade beneath mature tomato plants or bean teepees in hotter growing regions.

It should be noted that the success of any "intensive" growing plan is dependant upon adequate soil fertility and good garden management, as well as keeping pests at bay and harvesting crops to keep the plants in production. Knowing the growing conditions specific to your garden and what each plant needs to succeed is the key to getting the most out of your plot—be it large or small. Your reward will be more delicious, fresh, and healthy food.

BIBLIOGRAPHY

Emery, Carla, *The Encyclopedia of Country Living*, 10th edition, Seattle, WA: Sasquatch Books, 2008

Jones, Louisa, *The Art of French Vegetable Gardening*, New York: Artisan Publishing, 1995

Lloyd, Christopher, *Gardener Cook*, Minocqua, WI: Willow Creek Press, 1997

Pavord, Anna, *The New Kitchen Garden*, New York: DK Publishing, 1996

Solomon, Steve, *Growing Vegetables West of the Cascades: The Complete Guide to Organic Gardening*, 6th edition, Seattle, WA: Sasquatch Books, 2007

Botanical Interest: www.botanicalinterests.com
Renee's Garden Seed: www.reneesgarden.com
Southern Exposure Seed Exchange: www.southernexposure.com
Territorial Seed: www.territorialseed.com

INDEX

A

Acid soil, 26
Alfalfa, 30
Alkaline soil, 26
Amaranth grain, 110–11, 168
Angelica, 146
Artichokes, globe, 79–80, 168
Artichokes, Jerusalem, 8, 98, 168
Artificial fertilizers, 35
Arugula, 68, 168, 169
Asian radishes, 96
Asparagus, 8, 73–75, 168
Asparagus beans, 122
Aubergine, 134–35

B

Backyard wheat, 101–2
Balm, lemon, 147
Balsam pears, 130
Bamboo, 111, 168
Basil, 147
Bay, 148
Beans, 117–22
    interplanting, 110, 169
    maximizing your garden's yield, 167, 168, 169
    planning your garden, 5, 6, 7, 10, 11
    varieties and cultivation, 117–22
Bee balm, 148
Bee-attracting plants, 112, 148, 149, 154, 159
Beets, 10, 91, 169
Beginning gardeners, 5, 10–11
Bitter cucumbers, 130

Bitter melons, 130, 168
Black beans, 120
Bodi, 122
Bok choy, 65
Boonchi, 122
Borage, 149
Brionne, 130
Broad beans, 120–21
Broccoli, 81–82
    cultivation, 81–82
    maximizing your garden's yield, 168, 169
    planning your garden, 7, 10, 11
    soil enrichment, 30
Broccoli raab, 78, 168
Brussels sprouts, 6, 10, 64, 168
Buckwheat, 30, 112, 168
Bugs. *See* Insects
Bulbing onions, 54–57, 58
Bunching onions, 52, 169
Burnet, salad, 149
Bush beans, 5, 6, 117–18, 119, 120
Bush peas, 5, 115, 116, 117
Butterhead lettuce, 60

C

Cabbage, 6, 34, 62–63, 168, 169
Calabaza, 130, 168
Calabazilla, 130
Cantaloupe, 126
Cardoon, 75, 168
Carrots, 7, 10, 92–93, 169
Cassava, 90

Catnip, 150
Cats, 30, 39, 150
Cauliflower, 82–83, 168
Celeriac, 78, 169
Celery, 78–79, 169
Chaff, 103
Chamomile, 150
Chard
    cultivation, 70
    maximizing your garden's yield, 169
    planning your garden, 5, 7, 10, 11
Chayote, 130, 168
Chemical fertilizers, 35
Chervil, 151
Chile peppers, 137–38, 139, 168
Chinese black radishes, 96
Chinese cabbage, 65–66, 168
Chinese celery cabbage, 65
Chinese chives, 53
Chinese long bean, 122
Chinese mustard cabbage, 65
Chinese parsley, 151
Chives, 52–53, 168
Chocho, 130
Christophine, 130
Cilantro, 151
Citron, 124
Clay soils, 26, 28
Climate
    geographic zones, 22
    hill plantings, 16
    warm and cool-season plants, 7, 59, 167–69
    worm bin placement, 31
Cloches, 18, 81, 133, 134, 135
Clove type onions, 56–57
Clover, 30
Cold frames, 18–19
Collards, 7, 66, 169
Comfrey, 152
Common thyme, 160–61
Compact varieties, 10
Compost, 28–29
    asparagus, 74
    building a compost pile, 29
    cold frames, 18
    globe artichokes, 80

soil composition, 26, 34
    See also Manures; Worm bins
Container gardens, 5, 10–11, 148
Cool-season plants, 7, 59, 167–69
Coriander, 151
Corn, 104–9
    interplanting, 110
    maximizing your garden's yield, 168
    planning your garden, 6, 7, 11
    soil enrichment, 30, 34, 107
    varieties and cultivation, 104–9
Corn salad, 68–69, 168
Cos lettuce, 60
Coverings, gardens. *See* Garden coverings
Craft gourds, 131, 168
Crisphead lettuce, 60
Crop rotation, 41, 107, 115, 141
Crosne du Japon, 98
Cuban squash, 130
Cucumbers, 124–25
    cultivation, 124–25, 127
    maximizing your garden's yield, 168
    planning your garden, 6, 7, 10, 11
Curly parsley, 156

D
Daikon, 96
Daily harvesting, 11
Dandelions, 71
Dau gauk, 122
Deer, 39
Desert gardens, 16
Dill, 152
Dill seeds, 63, 152
Diseases, 39, 41, 81, 107, 141
    See also Insects
Double cropping, 10
Draft horses versus power tools, 14–15

E
Earthworms, 30–33
Edamame, 122
Eggplant, 7, 10, 133–35, 168
Elephant garlic, 56–57
Emery, Carla, ix–x, 163–64
Endive, 10, 71
English peas, 116

Erosion, 13
Escarole, 71
Experienced gardeners, 6, 10–11

F
Fabas, 120–21
Fava beans, 120–21, 169
Feeding mulches, 33
Fencing, 39
Fennel, 153
    See also Florence fennel
Fertilizer. *See* Compost; Manures; Soil
Fetticus, 68–69
Finnochio, 76
Flageolet beans, 120
Flails, 103
Floating row covers, 18
Florence fennel, 76, 168
Flowers, 7, 41, 79–83, 168
    See also specific variety
Foo gwa, 130
French tarragon, 160
Fuzzy melons, 131, 168

G
Garden coverings, 17–20
    advantages, 17, 20
    broccoli, 81
    eggplants, 134, 135
    hotbeds, 19, 63, 90
    loofah sponges, 132
    nightshades, 133, 134
    peppers, 134
    tomatoes, 140, 141, 142, 143
    types, 18–19
Garden layout, 13–17
Garden pests, 20, 39–41, 110
    See also Insects
Garden planning, 3–11
Garden record keeping, 8–9
Garden rocket, 68
Garden tools, 14–15, 37, 38, 103
Garden yield, maximizing, 167–69
Garlic, 8, 56–57, 63, 169
Garlic chives, 53, 168
German chamomile, 150
Giant cabbage/mustard family, 62–68
    See also specific variety

Giant lamb's-quarters, 70
Girasole, 98
Globe artichokes, 79–80, 168
Globe onions, 54–55, 168
Gophers, 40
Gourds, 123–32
    See also specific variety
Grain amaranth, 110–11, 168
Grasses and grains, 30, 101–13
    See also specific variety
Great Northern beans, 120
Greek oregano, 155
Green manure, 30, 103, 107, 112, 115
Green onions, 51–54
Green pumpkins, 130
Green tomatoes, 143
Greenhouses, 19, 23, 132, 133
Ground cherries, 143–44, 168
Groundwater contamination, 29, 35
Growing season, 23

H
Hairy melons, 131
Hand tools, 37, 38, 103
Harvesting, daily, 11
Herbes de Provence, 153
Herbs, 145–61
    planning your garden, 6, 8, 10
    use as insect repellant, 56, 63
    varieties and cultivation, 145–61
    See also Chives; Garlic
Hill planting, 16
Hoes, 38
Horticultural beans, 120
Hot peppers, 137–38, 139, 168
Hotbeds, 19, 63, 90
Hummingbirds, 148, 158
Husk tomatoes, 143

I
Iceberg lettuce, 60
Indian pumpkins, 130
Insects, 39, 41
    carrots, 92
    corn, 107
    cucumbers, 125
    garden coverings, 20

repellants, 41, 56, 63
tomatoes, 141
Irrigation. *See* Watering
Italian oregano, 155
Italian parsley, 156

J

Jack-o'-lanterns, 130
Japanese artichokes, 98
Jerusalem artichokes, 8, 98, 168
Jicama, 7, 99, 168

K

Kale, 6, 10, 66–67, 169
Kareli, 130
Kidney beans, 120
Knob celery, 78
Kohlrabi, 76–77, 168
Kudzu, 90
Kyona, 67

L

Lamb's lettuce, 68–69
Lavender, 153
Layout of garden, 13–17
Lead contamination, 27
Leaves, 7, 10, 59–71
    See also specific variety
Leeks, 53–54, 168
Legumes, 107, 115–22
    See also specific variety
Lemon balm, 147
Lemon thyme, 160–61
Lemon verbena, 154
Lettuce, 60–61
    maximizing your garden's yield, 168, 169
    planning your garden, 5, 6, 7, 10
    varieties and cultivation, 60–61
Loam, 28
Lobak, 96
Long beans, 122
Loofah sponges, 132
Looseleaf lettuce, 60
Lovage, 154

M

Mache, 68–69
Malanga, 90

Mango squash, 130
Manures, 29–30
    benefits, 28
    green manure, 30, 103, 107, 112, 115
    guidelines for use, 19, 29–30
    soil nutrients, 34
    See also Compost; *specific vegetable*
Marigolds, 41, 154
Marjoram, 155
Mediterranean salad, 68
Melons, 125–26
    cultivation, 125–26
    hand pollination, 127
    maximizing your garden's yield, 168, 169
    planning your garden, 7, 10
Mexican husk tomatoes, 144
Mexican parsley, 151
Mexican potatoes, 99
Mexican water chestnuts, 99
Mice, 40
Mint, 155
Mirliton, 130
Mizuna, 67, 168
Moles, 40
Mountain spinach, 70
Mulching, 13, 26, 33, 141, 152
    See also specific vegetable
Multiplying onions, 58
Mustard, 10, 34, 67, 168
Mustard/cabbage family, 62–68

N

Nappa cabbage, 65
Nettles, 71
Nightshade family, 133–44
    See also specific variety
Nitrogen
    beans, 110, 115
    carrots, 92
    corn, 106, 107, 110
    manure, 29
    peppers, 139
    pH analysis, 26
    soil nutrients, 34
    sweet potatoes, 89
Nonstarchy roots, 91–99

O

Oats, 112–13, 169
Okra, 7, 133, 135–37, 168
Onions, 51–58
    maximizing your garden's yield, 168, 169
    planning your garden, 5, 6, 8
    use as insect repellant, 56, 63
    varieties and cultivation, 51–58
Orach, 70, 169
Oregano, 155
Oriental chives, 53
Oriental eggplants, 134–35
Ornamental plants
    bamboo, 111
    beans, 119
    borage, 149
    cabbage, 62
    cardoon, 75
    chile peppers, 137
    chives, 53
    craft gourds, 131
    gardening under cover, 20
    herbs, 145, 146
    lavender, 153
    lemon verbena, 154
    lovage, 154
    okra, 135–36
    pot marigold, 154
    Rainbow chard, 70
    rhubarb, 77
    rosemary, 157
    sage, 158
    salad burnet, 149
    salsify, 99
    sea kale, 78
    thyme, 160–61

P

Pak choi, 65
Parsley, 156
Parsnips, 93–94, 168
Peas, 115–17
    maximizing your garden's yield, 168
    planning your garden, 5, 6, 7, 10
    varieties and cultivation, 115–17, 121, 122
Peat pots, 23–24

Peppers, 137–39
    maximizing your garden's yield, 167, 168
    planning your garden, 6, 7, 10
    varieties and cultivation, 133–34, 137–39
Perennials
    asparagus, 8, 73–75, 168
    bamboo, 111, 168
    bee balm, 148
    bunching onions, 52, 169
    cardoon, 75
    catnip, 150
    chives, 52–53, 168
    comfrey, 152
    eggplant, 134–35
    exotic squashes, 130
    fennel, 153
    French tarragon, 160
    garlic, 8, 56–57
    globe artichokes, 79–80, 168
    Jerusalem artichokes, 8, 98, 168
    lavender, 153
    lemon balm, 147
    maximizing your garden's yield, 168, 169
    mint, 155
    multiplying onions, 58
    nightshade family, 133
    peppers, 137
    pigeon peas, 168
    pineapple sage, 158
    planning your garden, 8
    purslane, 71
    rhubarb, 8, 77, 168
    Roman chamomile, 150
    runner beans, 121
    salad burnet, 149
    sea kale, 78, 168
    shallots, 57
    thyme, 160–61
    top-setting onions, 58
    winter savory, 159
Pests, 20, 39–41, 110
    See also Insects
pH analysis, 26
Phosphorus, 34
Pigeon peas, 121, 168
Pineapple sage, 158

Pinto beans, 120
Planning your garden, 3–11
Planting dates, 7, 20, 21–24, 167–69
  See also specific vegetable
Plot size and shape, 5–6
Pole beans, 6, 110, 118, 119, 120
Pole peas, 115, 116
Pollination, 106, 108, 127, 142
Popcorn, 6, 105
Pot marigolds, 154
Potassium, 34
Potato onions, 58
Potatoes, 6, 86–87, 168
Poultry, 39
Power tools versus draft horses, 14–15
Pumpkins, 10, 128–30
Purslane, 71, 168

Q
Quinoa, 113, 168

R
Rabbits, 39
Raccoons, 39
Radicchio, 71
Radishes, 6, 10, 94–96, 168, 169
Raised beds, 13, 15, 16
Rakes, 38
Rapini, 78
Rats, 40
Rat-tail radishes, 96
Record keeping, 8–9
Red wigglers, 32
Rhubarb, 8, 77, 168
Rocket, 68
Romaine lettuce, 60
Roman chamomile, 150
Roots, 7, 85–99
  See also specific variety
Rosemary, 157
Rototillers, 14–15, 37
Row planting, 14, 15
Runner beans, 7, 121, 168
Russian kale, 66
Russian tarragon, 160
Rutabagas, 97–98, 168
Rye grass, 30

S
Sa gord, 99
Sage, 158
Sakurajima, 96
Salad burnet, 149
Salsify, 99
Sandy soils, 25, 28
Savory, 159
Scallions, 51, 54, 55, 168
Scorzonera, 99
Scoville heat scale, 138
Sea kale, 78, 168
Seed packet planting, 20
Seed potatoes, 88
Shallots, 57, 169
Shell beans, 119–20
Shelling peas, 116
Shocks, 103
Sincama, 99
Sloped gardens, 13
Slugs and snails, 40
Small gardens, 5, 6, 10–11
Snap beans, 117, 119, 121
Snap peas, 116
Snow peas, 116
Soil
  chemical fertilizers, 35
  cold frames, 18–19
  earthworms, 30–33
  lead contamination, 27
  mulching, 13, 26, 33, 141, 152
  nutrients, 34
  pH analysis, 26
  sandy versus clay soils, 25–26, 28
  See also Compost; Manures
Solar power greenhouses, 19
Sorrel, 71
Southern beans/peas, 122, 168
Southern gardens, 7
Soybeans, 122, 168
Spades, 38
Spading forks, 38
Spaghetti squash, 131
Spinach
  cultivation, 69
  maximizing your garden's yield, 167, 168, 169
  planning your garden, 7, 10

Squash, 128–32
    hand pollination, 127
    interplanting, 110, 169
    maximizing your garden's yield, 167, 168, 169
    planning your garden, 5, 7, 10, 11
    varieties and cultivation, 128–32
Starchy roots, 86–90
Starting transplants, 23–24
Stems, 7, 73–79
    See also specific variety
Straw, 103
Straw bed planting, 86–87
Strawberry tomatoes, 143
Succession planting, 167
Summer savory, 159
Summer squashes, 5, 11, 128, 168
Sunchokes/sunroots, 98
Sunflowers, 11
Sunlight, 4, 10, 11
Swedish turnips, 97–98
Sweet balm, 147
Sweet bay, 148
Sweet corn, 105
Sweet fennel, 76
Sweet marjoram, 155
Sweet peppers, 138, 139, 168
Sweet potatoes, 7, 89–90, 168
Swiss chard
    cultivation, 70
    maximizing your garden's yield, 169
    planning your garden, 5, 7, 10, 11

T
Taro, 90
Tarragon, French, 160
Temperature. *See* Climate
Threshing, 103
Thyme, 63, 160–61
Tips for small gardens, 5, 6, 10–11
Tomatillo, 144, 168
Tomatoes, 139–43
    maximizing your garden's yield, 167, 168, 169
    planning your garden, 5, 6, 7, 10
    varieties and cultivation, 139–43
Tools, 14–15, 37, 38, 103
Top-setting onions, 58
Topsoil, 13

Transplants, starting, 23–24
Tree onions, 58
Trowels, 38
True celery, 79
Turnip-rooted celery, 78
Turnips, 97–98, 168

V
Vegetable pears, 130
Vegetable spaghetti, 131
Vetch, 30
Voles, 40

W
Walking onions, 58
Warm-season plants, 7, 59, 167–69
Wasabi, 96
Watercress, 161
Watering
    benefits of organic fertilizers, 28, 35
    liquid fertilizer, 33
    planning your garden, 4, 11
    soil composition, 25, 26
    starting transplants, 23, 24
    worm bins, 32
Watermelon, 126
Weather. *See* Climate
Weeds, 37
    compost piles, 29
    controlling, 14, 33, 37
    hand tools, 38
    row planting, 14, 106
Welsh onions, 58
Wheat, 101–3, 169
Windy gardens, 13, 16
Winnowing, 103
Winter artichokes, 98
Winter savory, 159
Winter squash, 128–29, 168, 169
Wong bok, 65
Worm bins, 30–33

Y
Yam beans, 99
Yams, 90
Yard-long beans, 122, 168

No home—whether city or country or somewhere in between—should be without *The Encyclopedia of Country Living*

THE ENCYCLOPEDIA OF COUNTRY LIVING
10th Edition
Carla Emery

With over 650,000 copies sold, *The Encyclopedia of Country Living* is the original manual of skills and country wisdom for living on the land.

928 pages • paperback • $29.95

Grow Your Garden *with* Sasquatch Books

WHEREVER BOOKS ARE SOLD

SASQUATCH BOOKS
www.sasquatchbooks.com